Penguin Handbooks
A Wine Primer

André Simon was born in Paris in 1877. He was married
in 1900 in London, where he lived off and on until his
death. In charge of the export sales of an important French
wine firm he gained considerable experience in both home
and foreign markets. His hobby was writing books about
wine: the first to be published was *A History of the
Champagne Trade in England* (1905); this was followed by
A History of the Wine Trade in England, in four volumes
(1908–10). In 1933 he ceased to have any commercial
interests in the wine trade and he founded the Wine and
Food Society – 'to bring together and serve all who take
an intelligent interest in the pleasures and the problems
of the table'. Besides editing and publishing the Society's
quarterly magazine *Wine and Food*, and visiting the Society's
many branches in various parts of the English-speaking
world, André Simon wrote and published a number of
books on gastronomy and on wine, the most popular of
them being *A Wine Primer*. He died in 1970.

André Simon

A Wine Primer

Revised Edition

 Penguin Books

Penguin Books Ltd, Harmondsworth,
Middlesex, England
Penguin Books Australia Ltd, Ringwood,
Victoria, Australia
Penguin Books Canada Ltd,
41 Steelcase Road West,
Markham, Ontario, Canada

First published by Michael Joseph 1946
Revised edition published 1970
Published in Penguin Books 1973
Reprinted 1974

Made and printed in Great Britain by
Cox & Wyman Ltd, London, Reading and Fakenham
Set in Monotype Bembo

Contents

6 Contents

Foreword

Air, food and water are indispensable: nothing else is. There is, of course, much else that is highly desirable, but not indispensable: wine and milk, for instance. The Chinese drink no milk; Moslems and Hindus drink no wine, and the same may be said of a considerable proportion of the population of other countries. But there is a difference: Moslems and Hindus are not allowed to drink wine; but we are free to drink what we please, but there are some who do not care for wine, and others who love it but cannot afford it. Wine is the best form of drink for civilized people – that is to say, people whose senses are trained and disciplined, trained to appreciate that which is best without the danger of their appetite getting out of control. For such people as these, wine is best. It is best because it is the most natural of all the drinks which man has contrived to prepare for himself; it is also the one with the greatest measure of individuality, the oldest form of beverage and the most universally accepted, if we except water, which is not a drink, like wine, beer or cider, imagined by man in his quest for happier days on earth.

Wine is the suitably fermented juice of freshly gathered grapes. Grapes grow practically everywhere except in arctic regions, but they demand too much attention and do not reach the right degree of ripeness to be worth anybody's trouble to grow commercially for wine-making in lands where summers are not dependable, as in England, or where they are too fierce, as in the tropics. In Europe, the northern limits of wine-making vineyards are, from west to east, Brittany, Normandy, Picardy, Flanders, the Rhineland north of Koblenz, and the northern plains along the course of the Danube. The southern limits are the waters of the Mediterranean, including many island vineyards. In Africa there are flourishing and very extensive vineyards at the two extremes of the continent; in the north, from Morocco to Tunis, through Algeria, and in the south, at the Cape of Good Hope, and for many miles inland. There are also vineyards at Nairobi, directly under the equator, and outside Johannesburg, in the Transvaal, but they are very small, an experiment or a hobby, but not commercial ventures. In America the largest vineyards and the best wines are found on the western or Pacific coast, from California and Mexico in the north, to Chile in the south, and the Argentine, the largest and best vineyards of which are on the eastern slopes of the Andes. On the Atlantic side, there are vineyards and there is wine made in Canada, in the State of New York and other eastern states of the U.S., as well as in Brazil and Uruguay. In Australia there is much wine made in New South Wales, South Australia and Victoria, and there are also vineyards of more modest importance in some of the other states. In Asia Minor there are vines growing all along the shores and in the islands of the eastern Mediterranean, in Palestine, Syria, Lebanon, Armenia, as well as in Persia and the Asiatic provinces of the U.S.S.R. Although Asia is now the least important of the continents as regards its vinelands, it can claim to have been the first to produce wine, since it was on Mount Ararat that Noah's Ark came to earth, and it was on the slopes of Mount Ararat that Noah planted the first recorded vineyard.

In the making of wine man interferes as little as possible with the course of nature, which is the reason why every wine is different, possessing an individuality of its own in a very much more marked degree than any other beverage made in large vattings, be they beers or spirits, and so blended and reblended and 'averaged' that he who has a thirst but no imagination may be sure that the label to which he has become accustomed is a guarantee that the beer or spirit in the bottle is identical to that which the same label has served to identify year after year. There are, in different types of wine, such as Claret and Burgundy, Sauternes and Chablis, Hocks and Moselles, and the rest, a family likeness, of course, but the members of each family all have their own features and moods, which vary from vintage to vintage, according to the differences in the hours of sunshine and inches of rain which the grapes get each year. That is not all. After the wine has been made – that is to say, after the grapes have been pressed and their sweet juice has been left to ferment – the natural process which transforms the sweetness there is in grape juice into alcohol and carbonic acid gas – it is but a green wine which must be given time to show its worth or the lack of it. The cask in which the new wine is lodged must be kept full to the bung, so that there shall be no excess of air having access to the new wine: it must be protected from draughts, extremes of heat and cold. Presently the wine in the cask reaches bottling status: it has discarded and thrown out what it did not need any longer, chiefly tartrates which form the lees at the bottom of the cask; it can be bottled and binned away to mature slowly with the merest fraction of air, which reaches it through the porous texture of the cork. Slowly but surely the wine in each bottle will grow softer and better, up to the time when it will begin to grow flat and bitter: it is then quite unfit to drink. To the spirit drinker, whose tipple is always the same, this glorious uncertainty of what the wine is going to be like, from one bottle to another, from one month to the next, may be a nuisance. But the wine lover does not always drink the same wine, and he does not care for the same wine from the same bin to be inevitably, monotonously the same, like a patent medicine. He tries one wine one day and another the next; he tastes with the utmost care, and pleasure, one bottle from one bin one day and another bottle from the same bin on another occasion, and he notes with joy any improvement or with dismay any sign of decay. Of course, in the latter case, he never hesitates but gives the doubtful wine no further chance to become too old. In the case of wine, age is not a matter of years: some wines will retain their youth and go on improving for many years, while a wine from the very same vineyard, but made in a less favourable vintage, will go to pieces after a very short term of residence in bottle.

Wine is never monotonous, and he or she who will only take the trouble to look for it should be able to find just the right wine for the right company and occasion. There are wines of many hues from the palest amber to the deepest purple; there are still and sparkling wines, and yet others which are just lively, not quite still and not really sparkling; there are dry and sweet wines, a whole range of fine shades and degrees of sweetness; there are wines which contain so little alcohol that any tee-totaller could drink them with a clear conscience, and there are also wines which are so potent that they must not be quaffed but sipped; there are wines which are quite delightful to drink freely within a year to two of their vintage, while others may live up to twenty-five, fifty, and even to a hundred years and still be a real joy for wine connoisseurs.

There is but one rule which needs to be remembered as regards the choice of different wines for different meals and occasions: 'The best wine is that which is the most suitable, hence the most pleasing at the time.' There are many rules concerning the service of wine, but none of them are binding, although most of them are reasonable. It is reasonable, for instance, to serve a bottle of a sweet white wine with a sweet dish, at the end of a meal, rather than with a roast grouse or a pork chop. It is reasonable to choose lighter wines to begin with and stronger, heavier wines to follow rather than to precede them, but the most reasonable thing of all is to find out what your guests would like and, if you have no guests, to make up your own mind what you think would be the most suitable, hence the best, wine.

Last, but by no means least, wine is best because it is the safest, pleasantest and most wholesome of all beverages. It is safer than water or milk: you cannot get typhoid or TB from any wine, be it old or young, cheap and nasty, or rare and costly. No microbes live in wine. It is pleasanter than other safe drinks because it is more gentle as well as more varied. There is no wine without any alcohol, since grape juice does not begin to be wine until it has fermented, and by then the sugar of the grape juice has become the alcohol of the wine. But the alcohol in wine is as the canvas upon which an artist paints a picture: it is there, of course, but you do not see it and do not think of it; it is not the canvas that you are interested in, but the picture which is on it. It is the same with wine; it is not the small percentage of alcohol that appeals to you, but the brilliant ruby of the wine's colour, the attractive perfume of its bouquet and the delicious savour of its farewell, the lingering taste which it leaves behind as it descends smoothly down your grateful throat: that is the picture that is painted on the canvas of the wine's alcohol. Of course the alcohol is there all the time, and very welcome it is: it holds everything so well together; it diffuses such a comforting light and warmth; it provides the limelight which enables us to enjoy fully all the fine points of the wine's colour, bouquet and flavour. And it does it in a gentle fashion; it is never brutal; it never is treacherous, stabbing one in the back or in the brain as immature spirits do. Wine is 'a good familiar creature', as Shakespeare calls it, and Shakespeare always is right. Wine is a gentle stimulant, a good counsellor, a true friend, who neither bores nor irritates us: it does not send us to sleep, nor does it keep us awake; it never becomes a craving or a tyrant; it is always ready to cheer, to help, but not to bully us.

Wine is a friend, wine is a joy; and, like sunshine, wine is the birthright of all. It grows so freely and is so cheap that there is wine for all, rich and poor alike, in wine-producing lands and in many others.

Aperitif Wines or Wines Served before Meals

The wines which are best served before meals may be classed into three main groups, in the first of which we shall place all *Dry Sherries*, in the second *Vermouths*, and in the third those registered brands of wines which may be called medicated rather than doctored – that is to say, wines made up to a prescription in which quinine or some spices, herbs, barks or roots monopolize all the limelight and leave none at all to the wine itself. The wines of all three groups serve, in the main, the same purpose, which is to sharpen the appetite and to stimulate the flow of gastric juices, helping us thereby to derive both greater pleasure and greater benefit from our meals.

One must never lose sight of the fact that he who is well nourished – fighting fit – is not he who eats most, but he who digests best. Appetite helps digestion. Appetite is not a luxury: it is a necessity, and one that is as pleasant as it is desirable. Hunger is quite another thing: it is neither desirable nor pleasant; it is a painful craving for food that is overdue. Appetite, on the contrary, is a keen but by no means brutal desire for food, coupled with a pleasurable anticipation of approaching satisfaction.

Aperitif wines – *apéritif* being a French word from the Latin *aperire*, to open – are served at the beginning or opening of the meal to prepare the way; they are not highly alcoholic nor should they be sweet, but possessed of a certain degree of sharpness, sometimes to the point of bitterness, which has the stimulating quality of a cold shower bath on a sultry summer's day. Their function is that of the clarion call bringing to attention taste buds above and gastric reserves below.

Aperitif wines are not a modern discovery or institution:

Greeks and Romans were partial to them long before the Christian era, and some of their aperitif wines would certainly fail to commend themselves to us, although they apparently served their purpose at the time. They used wormwood and aloes, which are still used now for the same purpose, but they also added to their wines asafoetida, myrrh, tar, sea water, pepper and spikewood, which it is difficult for us to reconcile with our present-day standards of good taste.

To get up from one's desk only just in time to sit at the dinner table is sometimes inevitable, but it is wrong. When brain or muscles have been in action, as they are when we are at work or at play, there should be some interval for relaxation before we begin our meal, and this is one of the reasons why the practice of serving an aperitif wine before meals has been so generally accepted for so long among all civilized peoples. Besides the beneficial action of the wine itself, the transition period of relaxation which it renders necessary between work and food is also of real benefit. This is why aperitif wines should never be tossed down like a nip of Vodka or Aquavit, but sipped in a leisurely fashion and, whenever possible, in the company of friends. This does not mean, however, that one should be surrounded by people more hospitable than sensible, who will not take 'no' for an answer but insist on calling for one more round: such people are well meaning but not real friends, since it is obvious that moderation must be the rule with aperitifs: appetite is a highly strung steed; the crack of the whip – just one glass – is all that is needed to get it to the winning post: if hit, it will bolt and run away with the rider.

I. SHERRY

Sherry is the wine of Jerez, in the south of Spain. That is why it is called Sherry, an anglicized form of Jerez.

Sherry is a white wine with the tan of fair sun-bathers. It is a white wine because it is born of white parents, made from white grapes, and, like all white wines, Sherry is best served cool, not iced, but at the temperature of a cold cellar; when there is no cold cellar in which to keep Sherry, a short stay in the ice chest will soon bring a dry Sherry to the crisp-cold temperature which is best for all white wines.

Sherry is a self-willed wine which gives a good deal of trouble to its guardians during its early years: it must have its own way, but, like many a difficult child, when Sherry reaches the age of sweet reasonableness, it is the most amenable of all wines, the best tempered, the most accommodating, the only one that will not let its nose be put out by being left overnight and even for some days in a decanter; the only one to put up cheerfully with cigarette smoke and over-scented women.

The white grapes from which the best wines of Jerez are made are very small and very sweet; they are borne in thick clusters by vines which are trained low so that the grapes get the benefit of the sun's rays during the day and of the heat from the baked earth at night. When they are ripe, these grapes are picked, and great baskets are filled with them. Mules bring them to the press-house to be emptied and then they are sent back to be re-filled. The grapes are not necessarily pressed as soon as they are picked. When the weather is suitable, they are spread on straw mats, covered with rushes or dry grass at night, to protect them from the dew, and uncovered again as soon as the sun shines in the morning. In this way they lose a little moisture, through sweating in the sun, but none of the sweet juice within each berry. They are then quite ready for the press.

In the Jerez country the wine-press is always set in the coolest barn of the farm, usually a long building with thick walls and mere slits to let a little light in but none of the heat of the sun. The press is called a *lagar*; it is about 10 feet square and made of stone; it holds about 1,500 lb. of grapes. When the *lagar* is filled with ripe, sun-dried grapes it is customary to sprinkle over them about 10 lb. of *yeso*, a form of gypsum, which is some of the chalky soil of the vineyards, but baked to a dust. This practice is peculiar to the *vignerons* of Jerez, who claim that this form of liming is helpful during the initial stages of the vinous fermentation, and that it is also responsible for the particularly dry 'finish' or after-taste of Dry Sherries.

When the *lagar* is full of ripe and limed grapes, a gang of disreputable-looking but probably quite harmless fellows get into the *lagar* and begin to tread the grapes. They wear specially made clogs, and as they stamp about the *lagar* they soon reduce to a sticky mess those 1,500 lb. of white grapes. It is reckoned that it takes ninety days and nights, mostly sunshiny days and heavily dewed nights, for the grapes to reach maturity from the time of the flowering of the vine; it takes about nine hours to tread and crush them under foot so that there is no juice left in them. A short life indeed and an inglorious death, but the grapes of Jerez do not die in vain; their sweet juice liveth again, as wine, and it liveth for four score and ten years, and even longer. This is the miracle of fermentation.

Fermentation is a perfectly natural phenomenon and like most of nature's work, it is naturally perfect. Fermentation is not merely natural, it is inevitable – that is to say, when and if grape juice is left alone. Man can and does interfere with this, as with so many other natural processes, to check it after a time, or even to prevent it making a start at all.

All ripe grapes contain some form of sugar in solution in water within each little berry, while the fine grey down on their skin consists of microscopic fungi, patiently queuing up outside awaiting their chance to get at the sugar within the grapes, and their chance comes when the grapes are crushed; they no sooner get mixed up with the sweet juice of the grapes than the sugar in it goes all to pieces; it breaks up, loses some of its carbon and oxygen in the form of carbonic acid gas, which escapes into the air, and it settles down eventually in a more stable form known as ethyl alcohol or wine alcohol. By then grape juice has become wine. Other things also happen during this process of fermentation, but the most important of all is this change-over from grape sugar to ethyl alcohol, and from grape juice to wine.

This is but the first lap of a long race, the first of the many stairs that lead to the throne room. Grape juice which has gone through fermentation has become wine, but not yet Sherry. In Spain it is called *mosto* or 'must', and it is a young child with a waywardness all its own, which makes it practically impossible

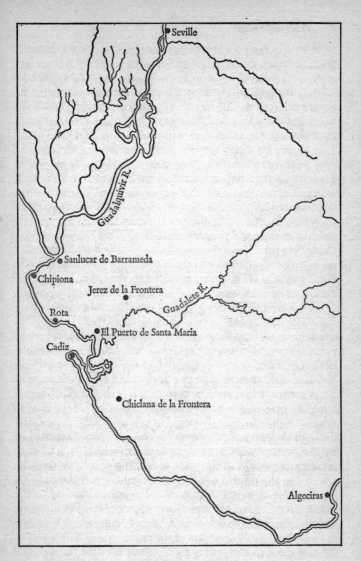

The Sherry District

to train it in the way one thinks best. Most other wines, when from six to ten weeks old, are amenable to expert guidance, and may be depended upon to grow true to parental type, be it Claret, Burgundy, Hock or Champagne. You can sell it for future delivery and be sure that it will not let you down. But you cannot do that with the *mostos* or young wines of Jerez. Nobody can tell what they will turn out to be a year hence. Like all young wines they go on fermenting at a slow pace so long as there remain in the new wine traces of the sugar present in the original grape juice: this may last from twelve to eighteen months, at the end of which the wine that was known as *mosto* has acquired the name and status of *vino de añada* or 'wine of the year'. By then all fermentation is at an end and the wine has reached its right and proper personality. What is so curious and so entirely peculiar to the wines of Jerez is that whilst the wine in, say, a hundred casks of *mosto* is to all appearances exactly the same, the wines in the same hundred casks of *vino de añada* will no longer be alike, so much so that it may seem hardly possible that all were made from grapes of the same species and of the same vintage. In one or two of those casks there may not be any wine at all, but vinegar; in two or three others there may be pricked wine on its way to the vinegar tube; these are the casualties to be buried or sent to hospital. In the rest of those original hundred casks there will be good wine, but by no means wine of uniform quality, style or type, and it is the work of expert tasters to grade the wine of each cask according to the class to which it will be found to belong. Casks in which the wine shows the highest degree of refinement, breed or elegance are chalked by the tasters with a two-prong fork, which is meant to represent a palm, and the wine so marked will henceforth be referred to as *palma*. In other casks the wine, good as it may be, may be lacking in the aristocratic or delicate character of the *palma*, but will have, in varying degrees, more body or vinosity, and the experts will mark each cask accordingly either with one or two plain, slanting strokes of the chalk, or else with a sort of slanting cross, one long stroke with a shorter one at the top. The wines in casks marked thus will henceforth be known as *raya* (one stroke), *dos rayas* (two strokes), or *palo cortado* (crossed).

When the wines of one and the same vintage have thus completed their fermentation and have been sorted out according to their individual style, they are stored in what is called the *criadera*, or nursery, where they are given first of all a dose of brandy, or distilled Spanish wine, which makes it quite impossible for any of them to attempt any further bout of fermentation, however slight, and where they are also given time to settle down and mature during three or four years.

Why should fermentation prove so different and, one might say, so erratic at Jerez, when it is so much more dependable anywhere else? The answer is that wines differ in quality and style not only according to the species of grapes from which they are made; according to the geological formation of the vineyards where such grapes are grown; according to the inches of rain and hours of sunshine – and their incidence – from year to year; but also according to the nature of the ferments responsible for the fermentation of the grape juice at the vintage time and after. These ferments are vegetable microscopic fungi, the spores of which lie in the dust and mud until they find a suitable ground for showing what they can do in the way of rapid growth. There are ever so many different species of such yeast fungi, even more than there are species of the edible and poisonous fungi, which are so large that there is no need of a microscope for us to see them. Not only the difference but the importance of the part which the yeast fungi play in the making of wine is proved beyond argument by the fact that the same species of grapes, grown upon similar types of soil, in different parts of the world, produce entirely different wines, the difference being due to different fermenting yeasts, not exclusively but predominantly. In more recent times this fact has been so well recognized that the vintners of Australia and South Africa have imported from Jerez the local yeast and have used it most successfully to make in Australia and South Africa far better Sherry-type wines than they had been able to make before from the same grapes. The peculiarity of the Jerez yeast fungi is their extraordinary rate of growth during the second or later stage of the wine's fermentation; these microscopic yeast fungi grow so rapidly that they form quite a thin sort of crust or thick film which covers the surface of the wine in the cask, shutting out the outside air and thus reducing to a minimum the rate of fermentation of the wine.

Returning now to the nursery or *criadera*, the different wines in reserve – *palma*, *rayas* and *palo cortado* – are sufficiently matured and are awaiting the Sherry shipper's pleasure. His work is not merely to ship his wines to all parts of the world where there is a demand for them: that is the last and easiest part of his job. The various wines in his nursery are to him what various paints are to an artist – the materials he uses to paint a picture. He must choose the right proportion and kinds of the different wines of different vintages to make not one but a number of different pictures, or different Sherries likely to appeal to the taste as well as the means of different customers. To do this, the Sherry shipper blends his wines on what is known as the *solera* system. *Solera* is not a particular type of sherry, but the name of the blending process of all Sherries; and this is roughly how it works.

A number of butts* of a particular type of Sherry, and of the finest quality of that particular type, are laid down in the *bodega* as a basis, close to the *suelo*, or ground, hence the name *solera*. The next and the following years an equal number of butts containing younger wines are placed on top of the first, then of the second and, lastly, of the third tiers. Thus are built a number of *soleras* of wines of different types. One *solera*, for instance, will be a blend of *palma* and *rayas*, while the next will be made up of *rayas* and *palo cortado* wines, and in varying proportions, according to the taste and skill of the artist, the Sherry shipper. When he wants to make up a Sherry for shipment to one or the other of the markets of the world, he draws as much of the wine of the bottom-tier butts of one, two or more *soleras*, as he thinks fit, and by blending them together he pro-

---

* *Butts* are Spanish casks with two tapering ends; there are *butts* larger than others in Spain, but the recognized size in the British Isles is the 108-gallons *butt*, which is used for shipping Sherry.

duces a Sherry which is different from the wine of other Sherry shippers, a wine made to his own pattern as well as one which can be matched, or blended again, in exactly the same way if and when the demand arises. Whatever wine he draws from the bottom butts of any *solera* is immediately made good by the same amount of wine from the different butts of the tier immediately above, and the gap thus made in the second tier is also made good from the wine of the third tier. In this way the wine of any particular *solera* is constantly refreshed by younger wine and it never loses its original identity.

One sometimes sees a Sherry offered as *solera* 1860, or any other date, but such a date does not refer to any vintage: it means that the *solera* from which this particular Sherry was drawn had been first laid down in 1860 – or whatever date is mentioned. Sherry is so much a blend of blends, of different wines of different vineyards and of different years, that it is not sold under the name of any particular estate or château, nor with any mention of a vintage, but under the name of the shipper responsible for the blending, as well as the name of the type of Sherry which he has aimed at. Sherry may be and often is sweetened before it is shipped, but it is by nature a dry wine, which is why it is so much more popular as an aperitif wine than as a dessert wine. There are four main types of Dry Sherry, all of them suitable for serving before or at the beginning of a meal: they are known as *Fino, Manzanilla, Amontillado*, and *Vino de pasto*.

Fino is or should be a Sherry with the largest proportion of *palma* or finest wine; it is very dry, pale in colour, elegant, with sharp and intensely clean finish, but in no way bitter.

Manzanilla is the driest and palest Sherry of all, but not necessarily the best; it has an almost bitter finish which some people simply love, while there are others who cannot abide it.

Amontillado is perhaps the most popular of all dry Sherries; it is not so pale and not so dry as the other two, but it has a very attractive nutty brown bouquet and flavour of its own, although they are meant to approximate the bouquet and flavour of the wines of Montilla – hence the name *Amontillado*. Montilla is in the province of Cordoba, a long way from Jerez, and its wines were for a long time denied the right to be sold as Sherry; they now enjoy the privilege, but they are difficult to find in the ordinary course of commerce.

Vino de pasto: This is the least typical of dry Sherries and, as a rule, the least expensive. Its name means 'table wine', and it is an all-purpose kind of wine, equally acceptable before as at the beginning of a meal; it is usually pale golden in colour, and is better described as not sweet rather than as dry.

Such names, however, are merely an indication of the style of Sherry one may expect. They are no guarantee of actual quality. One has to look for this to the name of the firm responsible for the blending of the different wines used in the making of any particular type of Sherry. In the majority of cases the name is that of a shipper – that is to say, a firm usually with vineyards at Jerez, and always with *bodegas* and large reserves of wine in Spain, ancient *soleras* and well-filled *criaderas*. One must also bear in mind that it is not only possible for merchants in this country to import Sherries and blend them in their own way in order to offer to their customers types of Sherry different from and quite as attractive as any blended in Spain, but that such has been the practice of a number of English firms for many years past. Thus, for instance, the style of Sherry blended at Bristol and well known under the name of Bristol Milk, a name which is not a registered brand but the common property of all Bristol vintners, just as Fino and Amontillado cannot be the monopoly of any shipper or merchant. As there is no goodwill attached to a name which is common property, both shippers and merchants have registered brands under which they sell blends of their own, upon the excellence and individuality of which rest their reputations and fortunes.

The dry types of Sherry are bottled for the sake of convenience and distribution, but they are not kept in bottle to age and mature; they are meant to be ready for consumption when sold, and although the best Finos do gain in bouquet and body when aged in bottle, most dry Sherries have nothing or little to gain by being kept.

Sherry bottles should hold twenty-five liquid ounces of wine or ten glasses of Sherry, as neither the Sherry nor the drinker thereof has a fair chance with less than two and a half ounces per glass.

The Sherry Case

In 1968 the Sherry shippers of Jerez entered into legal action regarding the precise definition of Sherry. The plaintiffs were Showerings Vine Products and Whiteways, who sought an injunction saying that Sherry was not generic but a style and type of wine. The Sherry shippers of Jerez were thus defendants but at the same time counter-claimed and the case came before Mr Justice Cross in the Chancery Division in the law courts of England in early summer 1968.

The Sherry shippers of Jerez were seeking a position of protection as enjoyed by Port, Madeira and Champagne. Mr Justice Cross in his judgment stated that 'Sherry' on its own meant wine produced, matured and shipped from the Jerez districts of Spain. He added a qualification that through long usage he was prepared to allow the continuing use of the word 'Sherry' qualified by the following geographical adjectives: Australian, British, South African, Cyprus and Empire. These and only these were allowed to be used with the word 'Sherry'.

The above judgment covered labels and all forms of advertising.

II. VERMOUTH

Vermouth is the French rendering of the German 'Wermuth', the name of absinth or wormwood (*Artemisia absinthium*), a low shrub which grows practically in all parts of Europe. It is not a particularly decorative or handsome shrub, but its grey-green leaves possess a very pungent smell and they yield, when distilled, an essential oil which is highly perfumed. It is from the leaves of wormwood that the 'Green Devil', opalescent absinth, is distilled. The little yellow flowers of wormwood contains *absinthina*, a milder form of the same essential oil; it is not nearly so pungent, but its attenuated scent is all that is needed to give otherwise flavourless wines a pleasing as well as somewhat puzzling flavour. The flowers of wormwood have been used to make dull wines less dull during the past 2,000 years, if not longer, and this wormwood-scented wine is the direct ancestor of our modern Vermouth.

In England Vermouth is not a newcomer. It was imported from the Hanseatic ports, as wormwood wine, during the reign of Elizabeth I; and it was even made in England – as it still is being made today – in the days of Shakespeare. Sir Hugh Plat, who was born in London in 1552, the son of a brewer, gives us in his book, *The Jewel House of Art and Nature*, perfectly straightforward directions how to make 'Wormwood wine very speedily and in great quantities':

Take smal Rochel or Conniack wine, put a few drops of the extracted oil of wormwood therein, brew it out of one pot into another, and you shall have a more neat and wholesome wine for your body, than that wine which is sold at the Stilyard for right Wormwood wine. . . .

What Sir Hugh calls the 'right Wormwood wine' was Rhenish wine, with wormwood flowers steeped in it, which the German vintners brought to England and sold at the Stillyard, the house which they owned in London and used as their headquarters, just as the Bordeaux vintners owned and used the Vintners Hall, which still stands in Upper Thames Street, while the Stillyard has long since disappeared. And the 'Rochel and Conniack wines', which Sir Hugh recommends as a basis for his home-made Vermouth, would be the best for the purpose: they must have been then, as the white wines of the Charente still are to this day, thin and dry, far from attractive as table wines, which was why they were the first to be distilled, when proved to be the best for making Cognac Brandy.

Vermouth is made from any white wine of no particular character and flavoured with wormwood as well as a number of different herbs, spices, roots and seeds. The name has no geographical meaning, and Vermouth may be made anywhere and everywhere, but it has been made in France and Italy for a longer time and with greater skill than anywhere else.

Both the French and Italian Vermouths are sold in full-size (litre) bottles out of which barmen reckon to serve thirty glasses.

(a) French Vermouth

French Vermouth is not merely so called because it is made in France, but also because it conforms to a certain style of Vermouth which is distinctly drier than Italian Vermouth, drier as well as lighter in colour.

The basis of French Vermouth is white wine, mostly light, thin, white wines from the Midi or southernmost departments of France, wines known as *picpouls* and *clairettes*, which develop an almost rasping dryness as they mature. To correct this defect, it is customary to blend with *picpouls* and *clairettes* a third of white Algerian *grenache* to two of the others. This blend of white wines is allowed to mature for a couple of years, when it is blended in the proportion of eighty per cent white wine and twenty per cent *mistelles*. These *mistelles* are made by checking the fermentation of white muscat grape juice, soon after the vintage, by adding brandy to it: they possess thus the original sweetness of the muscat grape juice, unfermented, and the strength of the added brandy. This blend is not Vermouth, but what is called basic wine. It becomes Vermouth after it has been blended once more, and this time with a highly aromatic liqueur obtained by steeping the various flavouring agents according to secret formulae which are the jealously guarded secrets of all Vermouth shippers. It is assumed, however, that there are no less than forty different kinds of plants, roots, leaves, peels, seeds and flowers used in the making of the aromatic liqueur destined to flavour French Vermouth.

Flowers of wormwood and elder flowers are probably always used, and among other likely ingredients the following are the more probable: nutmeg, coriander, cinnamon, hyssop, sweet marjoram, angelica root, quinine bark, cloves, camomile, bitter orange peel, centaury, gentian and linden tea. The selected plants, spices, barks, and herbs are put in a large tank; this is then filled with the basic wine, which is drawn off after a month or so, when it is known as the infusion. This infusion is diluted with some more of the original 'basic wine', its strength is tested and brandy is added as and when necessary to bring up the alcoholic strength of the Vermouth to as near nineteen per cent of alcohol strength as is considered advisable. As a rule the Vermouth which is intended for home consumption, in France, is kept at an appreciably lower alcoholic strength than that which is prepared for export markets.

According to French law, Vermouth must not exceed nineteen per cent of alcohol by volume, nor be below ten per cent, and it must consist of not less than eighty per cent white wine.

French Vermouth is always lighter in colour than Italian Vermouth, but there are some which are darker than others, the darker colour being secured by the addition of burnt sugar or caramel. It is also very important that Vermouth should be clear, free from sediment or crust, although, like all wines, it contains some tartaric acid which in time tends to crystallize in the form of cream of tartar. In order to get rid of this before the Vermouth is bottled, the formation of cream of tartar is secured by refrigeration. The Vermouth is put in glass-lined vats where the temperature is rapidly lowered to almost freezing point; this is the surest and quickest method of removing practically the whole of its tartaric acid, after which it is filtered and bottled. All this takes from three to four years to achieve, so that French Vermouth, although not an old wine when it reaches the consumer, is by no means a raw or new wine.

In most of the world's markets French Vermouth is practically synonymous with Noilly-Prat, the French firm which has secured almost a monopoly of the export trade in French Vermouth during the past 150 years of its existence. It started its business life in Lyon, but it has now been established in Marseille for a great many years. In France the only other Vermouth which has a large popular appeal is that which is made in Savoy at Chambéry; it is called for under the name of *Chambéry*.

(b) *Italian Vermouth*

Italian Vermouth differs from French Vermouth chiefly in colour and sweetness: most of it is much darker as well as a good deal sweeter, and as it is not generally matured for quite the same length of time it should also be cheaper. Italian law demands that Italian Vermouth be made from white wine not less than one year old, as it takes about another twelve months for the basic wine to be aromatized, blended, filtered and bottled; Italian Vermouth is never less than two years old when it is sold. Its strength is, on an average, fifteen per cent of alcohol by volume, but there are some Italian Vermouths up to eighteen per cent of alcohol.

The majority of Italian Vermouths are made from the white wines of Pulia, wines which are or were as plentiful as they were inexpensive – rather common, characterless, dumb wines, not at all attractive as table wines, but very suitable as the foundation of Vermouth.

The process of infusion of the wine with a number of various herbs, roots, spices, etc. is very similar to that described for the making of French Vermouth, but it may be said that in the case of Italian Vermouth there is a higher percentage of quinine bark used than is customary in France. The darker colour is merely a matter of more caramel or burnt sugar, and the sweeter taste is due in the first place to the fact that the basic wine made from Pulia grapes has nothing like the austerity of the wine made from the *Picpoul* and other French grapes; in the second place, it is due to the higher proportion of *mistelles* which is used in Italy. Yet not all Italian Vermouth is very sweet; some firms have placed on the market brands of Italian Vermouth which closely approximate the relative dryness of French Vermouth.

The two Italian firms whose Vermouths enjoy the greater measure of popularity throughout the world are Cinzano and

Martini & Rossi, both from Turin. But there are others whose Vermouths are in good demand both in Italy and overseas. Such are, in alphabetical order:

G. B. Carpano, Torino	Fratelli Gancia e Cia., Canelli.
Conte Chazalettes & Ca.,Torino	E. Martinazzi e Cia., Torino.
G. Contratto, Canelli.	Mirafiore, S. A., Canelli.
Fratelli Folonari, Cambiano.	I. L. Ruffino, S.A., Cambiano.
Freund, Ballor e Cia., Torino.	Trinchieri, Brosio, S.A., Torino.

(c) *Vermouth Cocktails*

A small glass of chilled French Vermouth, plain or straight, is the best form of aperitif in the opinion of many wine lovers, but it is quite common to see people in France enjoy their French Vermouth in a long tapering glass, with iced water, as a long drink, and with a generous dollop of cassis, a very sticky blackcurrant syrup, which makes it a sweet drink, the kind of drink which one cannot imagine having any stimulating effect upon the gastric juices. In the British Isles and in the U.S.A. both French and Italian Vermouths are used to a much larger extent in the mixing of cocktails than straight, and here is a short list of the more popular forms of cocktails with a Vermouth content:

Martini: one half Gin and one half French Vermouth.

Dry Martini: two thirds Gin and one third French Vermouth; dash of bitters.

Very Dry Martini: three quarters Gin and one quarter French Vermouth; dash of bitters.

Sweet Martini: one half Gin and one half Italian Vermouth.

Bronx: One half Gin, one quarter French Vermouth and one quarter Italian Vermouth.

Manhattan: two thirds Rye Whiskey and one third Italian Vermouth; dash of bitters.

Rob Roy: One half Scotch Whisky and one half Italian Vermouth; dash of bitters.

One of the most acceptable forms of Vermouth Cocktail is that which is served in the West Indies and South America under the name of *Vermouth achampañado;* and this is how it is made:

Twist a small piece of lime into a 5-oz. glass, add cracked ice, $\frac{1}{2}$ a teaspoon of sugar, 2 oz. French Vermouth and then fill with seltzer water, stir a little, and drink it gratefully.

III. COMMERCIAL BRANDS OF APERITIFS

There are some popular brands of aperitif wines, made up to a prescription or formula on a commercial scale, that is to say, in considerable quantities, sufficiently considerable to justify the cost of extensive and constant advertising campaigns, the only form of advertising which is profitable, provided that ample supplies of the advertised product are available. This means that commercial brands of aperitif wines are made, and can be made only where there are very large supplies of inexpensive wines to be had, chiefly in southern France and northern Italy.

The names under which commercial brands of aperitif wines are offered to the public, the shape and size of the bottles in which they are sold, and their manifold excellences are no secret: they are pressed upon the notice of the public by posters and publicity. The formula or prescription according to which each one of the aperitif wines is brewed is, of course, and must remain, the jealously guarded secret of the owners thereof.

Beverage Wines or Wines Served during Meals

The bulk of the wines made every year from all the vineyards of the world are plain beverage wines meant to be drunk when anything from one year to five years old, at mealtimes, to slake one's thirst and help one enjoy one's food. Incidentally, let it be remembered that the food that nourishes is the food that is best digested, and that to enjoy one's food is not a matter of self-indulgence, but of good digestion and good health. In that respect beverage wines are very valuable indeed. They are mildly alcoholic and possess a gentle stimulating action upon the nerves of the stomach and other internal organs, but their chief value is their sapidity – that is, the combined attractions of their colour, savour and flavour, which enhance our appreciation of the food that we are eating at the same time.

Beverage wines are the most natural of all wines in this, that their fermentation is not assisted nor arrested nor interfered with in any way. They are either red, white or pink in colour, according to the colour of the grapes from which they are made. It so happens that there are more black grapes than white grown, and there are also more red wines than white. Pink wines are made from red grapes, the skins of which are not allowed to remain in contact with their fermenting juice long enough to be dyed a true red, but in many cases they are merely made by blending together red and white wines, with more white than red. There are also pink wines which are merely white wines coloured with cochineal or any other tasteless and harmless vegetable or animal dye.

Red wines are not better than white, nor are the white better than the red, and there are times and occasions when even their bastard brother, pink wine, may be more acceptable and enjoyable than either red or white. As there are more red wines than white, it is only natural that there should be – and there are – more bad red wines than bad white wines, as well as more great red wines than great white ones.

All the red beverage wines of the world approximate as well as they can to the two main standards set by Bordeaux and Burgundy. The red wines of Bordeaux, which have been known in England during the past eight hundred years under the name of Claret, may be said to possess a more feminine quality, and the red wines of Burgundy a more masculine one: they are like brother and sister, different but without one having any claim to being called 'better' than the other. Outside Bordeaux and Burgundy a red wine is considered to be of the Claret type when lighter in colour and body, and of the Burgundy type when of a deeper hue of red and greater alcoholic strength. The white wines of the world, other than the plainest, thirst-quenching and inexpensive wines which have little or no character of their own, are made to resemble as much as possible either the wines of the Rhine and Moselle – that is to say, light wines with a highly developed flowery bouquet; or the wines of Sauternes, the richest, most luscious of white wines; or else the wines of Chablis, light wines which have not the same volume of bouquet as the wines of Germany, and are quite dry, entirely unlike the wines of Sauternes; they possess, however, a personality of their own, the charm of which has never yet been within the reach of the many imitators which it has attracted.

I propose to consider all beverage wines, or table wines, the wines which are best served with food, under three main headings corresponding to their colours: (1) red, (2) white, and (3) rosé or pink. In the first or red division, I shall deal first with the wines of Bordeaux; secondly, with those of Burgundy; thirdly, with other European red wines; and, fourthly, with various red wines from non-European vineyards. In the second or white division, I shall deal first with the wines of the Moselle and Rhine; secondly, with the wines of Sauternes; thirdly, with the white wines of Chablis and the rest of Burgundy; and fourthly, with all other white wines from

European and non-European vineyards. In the third or pink division, I shall deal with all wines which are neither true red nor true white wines.

I. RED BEVERAGE WINES

(a) The Red Wines of Bordeaux

Many years ago, in the twelfth century, one of the richest feudal lords in Europe, the Duke of Aquitaine, left all his lands and his wealth to his only child, a daughter, Eleanor by name. She was too rich a prize to leave to some foreign prince to claim; so thought the then King of France, Louis VII, who married the girl himself. That was just where his troubles began. She made his life simply unbearable, so much so that Louis agreed to a divorce. She left him, but poor Louis was no better off. Eleanor went and married, in 1152, Henri Plantagenet, then Duke of Anjou; the following year, in 1153, he became Henry II, King of England, and Lord of the whole seaboard of France, from Dieppe to the Bay of Biscay, Brittany excepted: Normandy and Anjou were his by right of inheritance, and Saintonge, Aunis and Aquitaine by his alliance with Eleanor. Henry was indeed as favoured by fate as Louis was ill treated; he had the wealth, the lands and power which were in Eleanor's gift, and he had peace at home withal; he lived in England and she lived in the capital of her own realm, at Bordeaux. The king, her husband, visited her there, and it was at Bordeaux that her two sons were born, John and Richard the lion-hearted, both to be kings of England in their turn.

It was thus that Bordeaux and the whole of the vineyards which then, as now, were the chief wealth of Gascony became part and parcel of the English realm, the merchants of Gascony being English subjects, and their wines English wines during more than three centuries. From Rochelle came the cheaper kinds of white wines, and from the Rhine the better sorts, but it was to Bordeaux that everybody in England looked for pleasant, fresh, clear red wines, wines which must have been different from one another in many respects, although they had a general family likeness and were all known by the popular name of Claret.

In time, of course, Bordeaux returned to its natural allegiance and became French again for all time, But the popularity of Claret in England survived the loss of Gascony. It liveth still.

Claret is the English name of the red wines made within the limits of the Gironde department, or Bordeaux district. It is a descriptive name which has acquired after something like eight hundred years of current usage a geographical meaning. It is descriptive of a type of red wine the colour of which is true and brilliant; free from any pink, yellow, above all, blue, colouring matter such as is present in some red wines from less favoured vineyards. Claret is a geographical name in so much that it was the name first applied to the red wines of Bordeaux; also because it has been universally accepted in England and in many parts of the world where the English tongue is spoken as referring solely to the wines of Bordeaux and during a great many years to the exclusion of all other wines.

However, the mere fact that the name of Claret is so clearly understood by so many people all the world over to stand for a certain type of light, dry, red beverage wine, as produced at, and shipped from, Bordeaux during the past many centuries, makes it not only tempting but practically a necessity to use the name Claret as descriptive of the type of red wine made in many other parts of the world, wine which is as much like the red beverage wines of Bordeaux as soil, climate, and other factors will permit. There is a very great difference between a wine described as 'Spanish Red', for instance, and another offered as 'Spanish Claret'. The first conveys but a very vague idea to the would-be consumer's mind, while the other is quite clear; it stands for a table wine, a wine that should prove acceptable as a beverage wine, during meals, with or without added water, to slake one's thirst. It is that sort of wine and no other; it is unsuitable before or after meals, as an aperitif or dessert wine. All this is made positive by the mere use of the name Claret, and there is no other name to take its place. That being the case, it

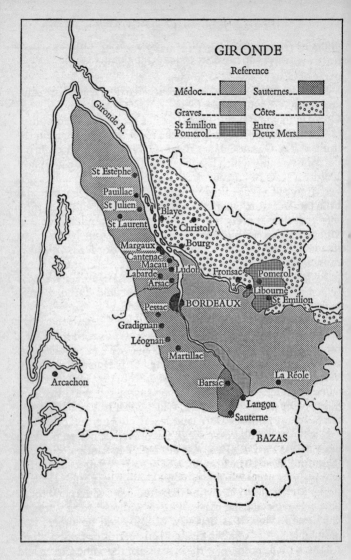

The Vineyards of Bordeaux

would be unreasonable to restrict the use of the name Claret to the red wines of the Bordeaux vineyards alone, but one should insist that when used, for want of another name, in connection with the red wines of other lands, the geographical name should always be coupled with the name Claret. If not, if a wine be offered under merely the name 'Claret', the inference is that it is a Bordeaux wine and the purchaser would have every right to refuse to pay for a wine sold to him merely as 'Claret', a wine which he is entitled to assume must be a Bordeaux wine, should such a wine be the produce of any other vines but those of Bordeaux. It is only if the seller makes it plain that the wine he is selling is a red wine of a Claret type but from Spain, South Africa, Australia, Algeria, or anywhere else, that he can be acquitted of all intention to deceive. In such a case the use of the name Claret, coupled with the country of origin, may be regrettable, but it is inevitable.

But how is it that Claret, real Claret, the red wine of Bordeaux, has been and still is such a favourite in every part of the civilized world? For it is a very, very long time ago since the bulk of the Bordeaux vintages were shipped to England; they have had for many years past, and still have, a considerable number of admirers not only in France, but in the United States, in Scandinavia, and practically in every corner of the world reached by civilization. No other wine has ever had such a universal appeal for so long as Claret. What is the reason for it? Probably because Claret approaches nearer to perfect harmony than any other wine.

One never tires of summer sunsets; they are always beautiful and yet they never are quite the same; it is ever the same delightful harmony without monotony. That is also the secret of the appeal which Claret has for all wine lovers; it is the most perfectly balanced wine and in ever a new garb; harmony without monotony. In other words, the two chief assets of all true Clarets are their perfect balance and their individuality.

There are other red wines, of course, which one may like as much as or better than the wines of Bordeaux, but none of the other vineyards of the world, which produce an abundance of red beverage wines, have to offer such a remarkable range of wines from the most inexpensive and get-at-able wines to the most expensive and exclusive.

The department of the Gironde, the Bordeaux district, produces every year an enormous quantity of Claret, most of which is good, pleasing, sound and wholesome wine and without any other merit than that of being much lighter and pleasanter than the rest of the red wines produced anywhere else in the world at the same price. But there are also, within the same department of the Gironde, large quantities of red wines produced, not every year but in many years, whenever the weather is favourable, which are not only quite distinctive but of outstanding merit. They all have a family likeness, of course, but they also have a personality of their own, a personality which adds greatly to their intrinsic value in the eyes of the connoisseur. This is why all the better-class Clarets are never blended together, as is the case with the wines of Oporto, Jerez or Champagne. Those are wines which reach the public under the names of men, women or firms responsible for the blending of a number of different wines from different vineyards, within the limits of their own respective districts. But in the case of Claret there is no name of blender to back the reputation of the individual vineyard responsible for the grapes from which was made the wine inside the bottle. It is the vineyard that counts, because it is from the soil of each individual vineyard that the wine in the bottle draws its personality. The name of the vineyard, of the *Château*, *Clos*, *Cru* or *Domaine*, always comes first and matters most. Then comes the date of the vintage. That also is very important, since not even the best vineyards of all are able to produce in sunless years wine worthy of their proud tradition. The name of the bottler or of the shipper comes next. Such name is also of importance, since some bottlers and shippers are better than others, but it only comes third in order of importance and quite a long way behind the other two.

There are, within the department of the Gironde, three main territorial divisions producing the best Clarets of all; they are known as *Médoc*, *Graves* and *St Émilion*.

MÉDOC The Médoc is by far the most important part of the Gironde department as regards the quantity of fine Claret it produces. It consists of a long strip of slightly undulating land alongside the left shore of the River Gironde, of which many acres were under water or water-logged until comparatively modern times, that is to say until the eighteenth century, when they were drained by Dutch polder experts. Compared to the vineyards of the Graves and St Émilion districts, which were famous as far back as the time of the Roman occupation, the vineyards of the Médoc, the oldest of which have barely five centuries of history to their credit, are almost modern, but they have outdistanced their elders in yield and reputation.

A Claret which is offered for sale under the name Médoc or Haut-Médoc might well be a little better than the wine sold as Bordeaux or even Bordeaux Supérieur, the *appellations d'origine contrôlées et réglementées* accorded to the unspecified wines of the Gironde department, whereas 'Médoc' may be used only for wines from vineyards in the northern part of the Médoc, nearer the sea, and 'Haut-Médoc' for those of the southern vineyards, nearer Bordeaux. A Claret sold as Médoc or even as Haut-Médoc should be inexpensive and suitable as a thirst-quencher wine of no particular merit or character. Why? Because if it had any character or merit, it would have a name of its own, the name of the parish where it was born, if not the name of the vineyard which produced the grapes from which it was made.

There are in the Médoc some seventy *communes* or parishes in which a great quantity of Claret is made every year, Claret far from being uniform in type, since each one of those many parishes possesses different soils. Four of them enjoy a greater measure of popularity than the rest as producing most of the best Clarets: they are the *communes* of Pauillac, St Julien, Margaux and St Estèphe.

A Claret sold to the public under the name of Margaux, St Julien or St Estèphe – the three most universally known names of the Médoc *communes* – may be quite an attractive wine, but it is never likely to be a great wine; it is not likely ever to be more than an ordinary, plain and acceptable but not exciting

Claret. It is, or it should be, the wine made from vineyards situated within the bounds of the particular *commune* whose name it bears, but not from any of its most favoured vineyards. For in these as in every other *commune* of the Médoc, there are vineyards better than others, and a few better than the rest, every one of them having a name of which it is very proud indeed. The Claret known to the world merely as Médoc is a foundling; that which is known by the name of its *commune* is known by the name of its mother, but is fatherless; that which is a legitimate child is known by the name of its father – the vineyard.

The sixty best vineyards of the Médoc have been carefully placed in order of merit, as far back as 1855, into five classes. They are known as the *classed growths* of the Médoc, and they are responsible, on an average, for more than a million gallons of the finest Claret of all, every year. Besides these sixty aristocrats there are some hundreds of vineyards with their own place in the scale under different designations, such as *crus exceptionnels, bourgeois supérieurs, bourgeois, artisans, paysans,* every one of them jealous of its own name and fair fame; they produce on an average some eight million gallons of very fair Claret every year. Lastly the vineyards which produce the least admirable Claret are reponsible for over a million gallons of Claret every year, the wine which is sold under the name of one of the *communes* of the Médoc, or merely as Médoc or Haut Médoc.

The Classed Growths of the Médoc

These are of sufficient importance to the Claret lover to justify being set out here for future reference under three different forms, i.e. (1) the official list in order of merit, with the name of the château and the names of the *communes* in which they are situated; (2) the same châteaux or *crus* arranged geographically – that is, with the names of their communes first, as if one proceeded from Bordeaux towards the Bay of Biscay in a north-north-western direction, along the left bank of the Gironde; (3) alphabetically, with cross-reference to the other two lists.

Official Classification of the Growths of the Médoc

First Growths

Lafite-Rothschild	Pauillac
Margaux	Margaux
Latour	Pauillac
Haut-Brion	Pessac

Second Growths

Mouton-Rothschild	Pauillac
Rausan-Ségla	Margaux
Rauzan-Gassies	Margaux
Léoville-Las Cases	St Julien
Léoville-Poyferré	St Julien
Léoville-Barton	St Julien
Durfort	Margaux
Lascombes	Margaux
Gruaud-Larose	St Julien
Brane-Cantenac	Cantenac
Pichon-Longueville	Pauillac
Pichon-Longueville-Comtesse de Lalande	Pauillac
Ducru-Beaucaillou	St Julien
Cos d'Estournel	St Estèphe
Montrose	St Estèphe

Third Growths

Kirwan	Cantenac
D'Issan	Cantenac
Lagrange	St Julien
Langoa	St Julien
Giscours	Labarde
Malescot St Exupéry	Margaux
Cantenac-Brown	Cantenac
Palmer	Margaux
Grand-La-Lagune	Ludon
Desmirail	Margaux
Calon-Ségur	St Estèphe
Ferrière	Margaux
Marquis-d'Alesme-Becker	Margaux
Boyd-Cantenac	Margaux

Fourth Growths

Saint-Pierre-Bontemps et Sevaistre	St Julien
Branaire-Ducru	St Julien
Talbot	St Julien
Duhart-Milon	Pauillac
Pouget	Cantenac
La Tour-Carnet	St Laurent
Rochet	St Estèphe
Beychevelle	St Julien
Le Prieuré-Lichine	Cantenac
Marquis-de-Terme	Margaux

Fifth Growths

Pontet-Canet	Pauillac
Batailley	Pauillac
Haut-Batailley	Pauillac
Grand-Puy-Lacoste	Pauillac
Grand-Puy-Ducasse	Pauillac
Lynch-Bages	Pauillac
Dauzac	Labarde
Mouton Baron Philippe	Pauillac
Du Tertre	Arsac
Pédesclaux	Pauillac
Belgrave	St Laurent
Camensac	St Laurent
Cos-Labory	St Estèphe
Clerc-Milon-Mondon	Pauillac
Croizet-Bages	Pauillac
Cantemerle	Macau

Average Output of the Classed Growths of the Médoc

		Pre-war average yearly output (tonneaux)*	Post-war average output (tonneaux)
LUDON.	Grand-La-Lagune	60	20
MACAU.	Cantemerle	100	100
ARSAC.	Du Tertre	10	100
LABARDE.	Giscours	60	20
	Dauzac	60	60

* A *tonneau* is 210 gallons.

		Pre-war average yearly output (tonneaux)	Post-war average output (tonneaux)
CANTENAC.	Brane-Cantenac	150	100
	Kirwan	100	100
	D'Issan	50	30
	Cantenac-Brown	90	90
	Palmer	100	100
	Le Prieuré-Lichine	30	30
	Pouget	30	30
MARGAUX.	Château Margaux ter. Vin	150	150
	Rausan-Ségla	60	60
	Rauzan-Gassies	50	50
	Durfort	80	30
	Lascombes	35	35
	Malescot-St Exupéry	50	50
	Ferrière	20	20
	Desmirail	80	30
	Marquis-d'Alesme-Becker	25	20
	Boyd-Cantenac	25	20
	Marquis-de-Terme	75	75
SAINT-LAURENT.	La Tour-Carnet	50	70
	Belgrave	70	150
	Camensac	70	70
SAINT-JULIEN.	Léoville-Las Cases	160	125
	Léoville Le Clos du Marquis	40	25
	Léoville-Poyferré	120	120
	Léoville-Barton	80	100
	Gruaud-Larose	250	185
	Ducru-Beaucaillou	150	130
	Lagrange	200	100
	Langoa	100	75
	Saint-Pierre-Bontemps et Sevaistre	100	100
	Branaire-Ducru	100	100
	Talbot	150	140
	Beychevelle	160	100
PAUILLAC.	Lafite-Rothschild	150	180
	Latour	100	100
	Mouton-Rothschild	150	75
	Pichon-Longueville	78	78

		Pre-war average yearly output *(tonneaux)*	Post-war average output *(tonneaux)*
PAUILLAC.	Pichon-Longueville Lalande	100	100
	Duhart-Milon	140	140
	Pontet-Canet	200	200
	Batailley	50	80
	Haut-Batailley	0	40
	Grand-Puy-Ducasse	40	35
	Grand-Puy-Lacoste	120	70
	Lynch-Bages	130	100
	Mouton Baron Philippe	175	100
	Croizet-Bages	50	50
	Pédesclaux	40	50
	Clerc-Milon-Mondon	35	35
SAINT-ESTÈPHE.	Cos d'Estournel	150	150
	Montrose	100	100
	Calon-Ségur	225	150
	Rochet	100	60
	Cos-Labory	45	45

An Alphabetical List of the Classed Growths of the Médoc

Batailley	Pauillac	5th
Belgrave	St Laurent	5th
Beychevelle	St Julien	4th
Boyd-Cantenac	Margaux	3rd
Branaire-Ducru	St Julien	4th
Brane-Cantenac	Cantenac	2nd
Calon-Ségur	St Estèphe	3rd
Camensac	St Laurent	5th
Cantemerle	Macau	5th
Cantenac-Brown	Cantenac	3rd
Clerc-Milon-Mondon	Pauillac	5th
Cos D'Estournel	St Estèphe	2nd
Cos-Labory	St Estèphe	5th
Croizet-Bages	Pauillac	5th
Dauzac	Labarde	5th
Desmirail	Margaux	3rd
D'Issan	Cantenac	3rd
Ducru-Beaucaillou	St Julien	2nd
Duhart-Milon	Pauillac	4th

Durfort	Margaux	2nd
Du Tertre	Arsac	5th
Ferrière	Margaux	3rd
Giscours	Labarde	3rd
Grand-La-Lagune	Ludon	3rd
Grand-Puy-Ducasse	Pauillac	5th
Grand-Puy-Lacoste	Pauillac	5th
Gruaud-Larose	St Julien	2nd
Haut-Batailley	Pauillac	5th
Haut-Brion	Pessac	1st
Kirwan	Cantenac	3rd
Lafite-Rothschild	Pauillac	1st
Lagrange	St Julien	3rd
Langoa	St Julien	3rd
Lascombes	Margaux	2nd
Latour	Pauillac	1st
La Tour-Carnet	St Laurent	4th
Léoville-Barton	St Julien	2nd
Léoville-Las Cases	St Julien	2nd
Léoville-Poyferré	St Julien	2nd
Le Prieuré-Lichine	Cantenac	4th
Lynch-Bages	Pauillac	5th
Malescot-St-Exupéry	Margaux	3rd
Margaux	Margaux	1st
Marquis-d'Alesme-Becker	Margaux	3rd
Marquis-de-Terme	Margaux	4th
Montrose	St Estèphe	2nd
Mouton Baron Philippe	Pauillac	5th
Mouton-Rothschild	Pauillac	2nd
Palmer	Margaux	3rd
Pédesclaux	Pauillac	5th
Pichon-Longueville	Pauillac	2nd
Pichon-Longueville-Lalande	Pauillac	2nd
Pontet-Canet	Pauillac	5th
Pouget	Cantenac	4th
Rausan-Ségla	Margaux	2nd
Rauzan-Gassies	Margaux	2nd
Rochet	St Estèphe	4th
Saint-Pierre-Bontemps et Sevaistae	St Julien	4th
Talbot	St Julien	4th

Notes on the Classed Growths of the Médoc

First Growths. The three First Growths of the Médoc are four, since it was decided, in 1855, that Château Haut-Brion the finest Growth of the Graves District, should rank as the peer of Lafite, Margaux and Latour, the three First Growths of the Médoc proper. These four First Growths owe their proud place to the fact that their wines have proved to be more consistently reliable over a great number of years than any of the other wines of the Bordeaux vineyards. But it does not mean that they are necessarily better every year, nor that they are identical. The only factor which remains invariably in their favour is the nature of the soil – and the aspect – of their vineyards. But there are years when frosts or hail may visit and damage them and spare other vineyards near by. And there is also the most important and always uncertain human factor, that is to say, the more or less intelligent or skilled labour of the men in charge of harvesting the grapes, pressing them and attending to the making of the wine. This is why the wines of Lafite were the best in 1864, those of Margaux were first in 1869, while Latour had pride of place in 1875 and 1878 and Haut-Brion in 1871. These differences are not apparent until the wines are fairly old, and even then they are not very marked when the weather has been so fine that there has been no excuse for poor wine being made anywhere. But there are years when conditions are unfavourable and when, by greater skill or better luck than its peers, one château will succeed in making wine of much better quality than the rest. Thus in 1888, a year when mildew was widespread in the Bordeaux vineyards, Margaux managed to make a delightful wine when the others failed. In 1895 a very hot and much too rainless summer was responsible for hard and tanniny Clarets, except at Lafite, where they managed to make a very fine wine. In 1910, one of the coldest and wettest summers on record, Lafite, Margaux and Latour made such poor wines that they were sold as plain Médoc, not being deserving of bearing the illustrious names of their birth, and yet Haut-Brion managed to bring forth a wine which, while not one of its best, was nevertheless quite good enough to be sold as Haut-Brion. This means that among the four First Growths there is none deserving first place consistently: it all depends on the vintage. In more recent years Latour had certainly pride of place in 1920 and 1929, Haut-Brion in 1923, Lafite in 1924 and 1934 and Margaux in 1928.

How to tell one First Growth from the other is a more difficult matter to set down in cold print. It is chiefly a matter of fine shades of differences of bouquet, that faint, flowery fragrance which rises from the wine to meet the keen and expectant sense of smell. It might be said that the bouquet of the wines of Lafite has a discreet and pleasing perfume of violets, the wines of Margaux being more like that of wallflowers, those of Latour nearer verbena, and those of Haut-Brion more like mignonette.

Second Growths. At the top of the list of the Second Growths of the Médoc stands Château Mouton-Rothschild, and there are many good judges who are of opinion that this château should be among the First Growths. It is generally accepted that the Mouton-Rothschild 1875 was as fine as any of the wines of the First Growths of that year, that their 77 was better than that of the first Four, and so is today the Mouton-Rothschild 1949. The Bordeaux shippers, who back their judgement by hard cash, often pay as much and sometimes pay more for the wines of Mouton than for those of the First Growths.

Of the next two Second Growths, Rausan-Ségla and Rauzan-Gassies, the first enjoys, and deserves, a greater measure of popularity than the other: it is always good and often very fine.

Then come the three Léovilles, the vineyards of which stretch from those of Beychevelle to those of Latour: the largest holding belongs to Château Léoville-Las Cases, with an average yield of 125 tuns, whilst the next largest is that of Château Léoville-Poyferré, with an average yield of 120 tuns; the smallest being that of Château Léoville-Barton, with an average yield of 100 tuns. In England the wines of Léoville-Poyferré have enjoyed a greater measure of favour than those of the other two, the wines of Léoville-Barton being next in popularity.

Châteaux Durfort and de Lascombes were originally one and the same property: their wines are of the best.

Gruaud-Larose-Faure and Gruaud-Larose-Sarget were also originally owned by one and the same Mr Gruaud and his heir, a Mr de Larose, from 1757 until 1812, when they were purchased by the Baron Sarget, whose heirs sold about two thirds of the vineyards to a Mr Faure. However, in 1935 the then owner of Gruaud-Larose-Sarget bought the Gruaud-Larose-Faure, so that, beginning with the vintage of 1936, the wines of the former two châteaux have been sold under the name of Gruaud-Larose.

The Châteaux Brane-Catenac is a very modest building, very far from castle-like, but its vineyards are among the best of the Médoc, and its wines may be described as the younger brothers of those of Château Margaux, which they resemble.

The vineyards of Châteaux Pichon-Longueville and those of Château Latour are contiguous, and the wines of Latour beat those of Pichon-Longueville by a short head only in the majority of vintages. Soon after the Napoleonic wars, some three-fifths of the Pichon-Longueville vineyards were sold to the Comtesse de Lalande, and there have been ever since two Châteaux Pichon-Longueville, the older and smaller one, which retains the old name, and the more modern and larger one which is known as Château Pichon-Longueville-Comtesse-de-Lalande.

Château Ducru-Beaucaillou is one of the finest residences of St Julien, and its vines are among the choicest; its wines, which are not only beautiful when of a great vintage, but always dependable, gained a great measure of popularity in England during the years when this château belonged to Mr Nathaniel Johnston, and when its wines were marketed by his firm.

Cos d'Estournel and Château Montrose are the two finest *crus* of St Estèphe. Their vineyards are at no great distance just north of those of Château Lafite, and their wines are first cousins, by no means poor relations of their illustrious neighbour. As a matter of fact, the Cos d'Estournel 1893 was quite as fine, if not finer, than the Lafite of that vintage. Professor

Saintsbury refers to Montrose as 'one of the least common of the second growths in England, but charming at its best'.

Third Growths. Of the fourteen Third Growths no less than nine are in the adjoining *communes* of Cantenac and Margaux, Châteaux Kirwan, d'Issan and Brown, in Cantenac; Châteaux Malescot, Palmer, Desmirail, Ferrière, Marquis d'Alesme and Boyd, in Margaux. The Château Giscours, in the near-by *commune* of Labarde, may also be included in the Margaux group.

Of the remaining four Third Growths, two are in the *commune* of St Julien, and one each in the *communes* of Ludon and St Estèphe. Château Lagrange is by far the more important as regards the extent of its vineyards and their vinous yield. The other St Julien Third Growth, Château Langoa, and its vines were purchased by Mr Hugh Barton in 1821, and they still are the property of members of the Barton family, partners in the Bordeaux firm of Barton et Guestier. Château Calon-Ségur, the oldest château of St Estèphe, has the largest vineyards of the *commune*. The wines of Château La-Lagune or Grand-La-Lagune, the one and only classed growth of the *commune* of Ludon, have always been in good demand.

Fourth Growths. The most popular of the eleven Fourth Growths is Château Beychevelle. The château itself, rebuilt in 1757 on the site of one of the oldest feudal strongholds of the Gironde, is a noble and most attractive residence; its vineyards are extremely well cared for, and its wines are always dependable and often delightful. There are four other Fourth Growths in the *commune* of St Julien, Châteaux Talbot and Branaire-Ducru, and two Châteaux St Pierre, but both have been reunited under the same ownership since 1920.

The other Four Growths are Château Duhart-Milon, Pauillac; Châteaux Pouget and Le Prieuré-Lichine, Cantenac; Château La Tour-Carnet, St Laurent; Château Rochet, St Estèphe; and Château Marquis-de-Terme, Margaux.

Fifth Growths. The first of the Fifth Growths, Château Pontet-Canet, is better known all the world over than, perhaps, any other Claret. This is surely due to the business acumen of the

Cruse family, whose members have owned Pontet-Canet ever since 1865, and have spared neither money nor labour to make good wine and to make it known in most markets of the world; but it may also be due to the fact that they have for years refused to mark it 'château bottled', and also refused to prosecute unscrupulous dealers who sold, under the name of Pontet-Canet, Claret which was not entitled to the name. However, when one gets the real Pontet-Canet, which one does when dealing with the right type of wine-merchant, one can be sure of getting a sound and pleasant wine, always; one may also get, in particularly favoured vintages, a wine of rare excellence and every bit as fine as any of the Fourth, Third, or even Second Growths.

There are no less than ten other Fifth Growths in the same *commune* of Pauillac, the best known of them being Château Mouton Baron Phillippe. Of the remaining six Fifth Growths none are much in demand in this country, but one of them, Château Cantemerle, has of recent years gained a great measure of well-deserved popularity.

GRAVES   Next to the Médoc, the Graves district is the most important as regards the quantity of really fine Claret it produces. The generally accepted notion among the public is that the name Graves refers to a white wine. There is, of course, a great deal of white wine made from the vineyards of the Graves district, the strip of land that stretches from Bordeaux towards the south along the left bank of the River Garonne, as far as the Sauternes country; but there is more red wine, or Claret, made from those same vineyards than there is white. And what is of greater importance, there is far better red Graves than white. Good as some of the white wines of Graves may be, none of them can pretend to come anywhere near the same class as some of the red wines in point of superlative excellence.

Château Haut-Brion has long held pride of place as the finest red wine of Graves, and it still ranks as the peer of the three First Growths of the Médoc, but its wines have not been up to their ancient reputation every year during the past thirty years or so. There has never been any official classification of the Graves wines, such as exists for the wines of the Médoc, but among the finest red Graves the following châteaux or estates deserve to be remembered: Château Pape-Clément, Domaine de Chevalier, Châteaux La Mission-Haut-Brion, Haut-Bailly, Carbonnieux, and Smith-Haut-Lafitte.

Here is an alphabetical list of some of the better-known red wines of Graves:

Château or Estate	*Commune or Parish*
Barthez	Gradignan
Bel-Air	Talence
Bel-Air	Le Haillan
Bellegrave	Pessac
Boismartin	Léognan
Bouscaut	Cadaujac
Camponac	Pessac
Carbonnieux	Villenave d'Ornon
Chevalier, Domaine de	Léognan
Ferrand	Martillac
Fieuzal	Léognan
Haut-Bailly	Léognan
Haut-Brion	Pessac
Haut-Brion-Larrivet	Léognan
Haut-Gardère	Léognan
Haut-Madère	Villenave d'Ornon
Hermitage	Martillac
La Ferrade	Villenave d'Ornon
Lafon	Gradignan
Lagarde, Domaine de	Martillac
La Louvière	Léognan
La Mission-Haut-Brion	Pessac
La Tour-Kressmann	Martillac
Latour-Haut-Brion	Talence
Laurenzane	Gradignan
Malartic-Lagravière	Léognan
Pape-Clément	Pessac
Phénix-Haut-Brion	Pessac
Pique-Caillou	Mérignac

Château or Estate	*Commune or Parish*
Pontac-Monplaisir	Villenave d'Ornon
Portets, de	Portets
Rochemorin	Martillac
Smith-Haut-Lafitte	Martillac
Tauzia	Gradignan
Virelade, de	Virelade

The majority of the red wines of Graves differ from those of the Médoc and St Émilion by being rather sweeter, not sweet, however, in terms of sugar, but sweet in the sense of graciousness, not angular, hence more immediately appealing. They are also, as a rule, ready to drink at an earlier age than wines of the Médoc, yet they last quite as long.

ST ÉMILION To the north of Bordeaux, and upon the right bank of the River Dordogne, there are quite a number of important vinelands stretching in all directions from the old city of St Émilion. This is the third wine-producing district of the Gironde in point of quality, taking the whole of the Claret produced within the St Émilion area, and the second in point of quality of wine produced.

The wines of St Émilion are darker in colour and somewhat bigger of body than the Clarets of the Médoc, but they do not last so long. They show, when young, greater strength and promise of longevity, but they are rarely as exquisitely balanced as the best Médocs; hence their shorter span of useful life. The wines of St Émilion possess a bouquet which is quite distinct from that of the Médoc or Graves Clarets; it is chiefly vinous, of course, but it has just a faint and very pleasant fragrance which cannot be better described than rather like that of cedar wood.

The vineyards of St Émilion stretch from the very top of the hill, or rather plateau, of St Émilion itself, towards the River Dordogne, some four miles away. About half-way down the hill the soil of the vineyards is more gravelly and it produces Clarets which are known as 'Graves de St Émilion': they bear an unmistakable family likeness to the others, but they are rather softer in texture or more tender. As Château Ausone is the typical and best known St Émilion wine from the top of the hill, so is Château Cheval-Blanc the typical and best known Graves de St Émilion. Further away from the old church of St Émilion, as one proceeds towards the Dordogne, one comes to the extensive vineyards of Pomerol, which produce a large quantity of very charming Clarets, often sold as wines of St Émilion, although quite distinctive, rather firmer of body, and fully deserving to go into the world under the name of Pomerol

An alphabetical list of some of the principal *crus* of St Émilion and Pomerol:–

Château or Estate	*Commune or Parish*
Angélus, Clos del'	St Émilion
Ausone	St Émilion
Baleau	St Émilion
Beauregard	Pomerol
Beauséjour	St Émilion
Bélair	St Émilion
Bel-Air-Marignan	St Émilion
Bellevue	St Émilion
Berliquet	St Émilion
Cadet-Bon	St Émilion
Cadet-Priola	St Émilion
Canon	St Émilion
Canon-La-Gaffelière	St Émilion
Cap-de-Mourlin	St Émilion
Capdemourlin-Magdelaine	St Émilion
Certan	Pomerol
Cheval-Blanc	St Émilion
Clinet	Pomerol
Clos Fourtet	St Émilion
Commanderie, La	Pomerol
Conseillante, La	Pomerol
Corbin	St Émilion
Coutet	St Émilion
Couvent, Clos du	St Émilion
Curé-Bon-La-Madeleine	St Émilion

Château or Estate	*Commune or Parish*
Daugay	St Émilion
Dominique, La	Pomerol
Église, Clos l'	Pomerol
Église, Domaine de l'	Pomerol
Église-Clinet, Clos de l'	Pomerol
Figeac	St Émilion
Fonplégade	St Émilion
Fonroque	St Émilion
Fourtet, Clos	St Émilion
Franc-Mayne	St Émilion
Gaffelière, La	St Émilion
Gazin	Pomerol
Grand-Corbin	St Émilion
Grand-Mayne	St Émilion
Grand-Pontet	St Émilion
Grandes Murailles, Les	St Émilion
Grandes-Vignes, Clos des	Pomerol
Guillot	Pomerol
Haut-Cadet	St Émilion
Lacabanne	Pomerol
La Croix	Pomerol
La Croix-de-Gay	Pomerol
Lafleur	Pomerol
La Fleur-du-Gazin	Pomerol
La Fleur-Pétrus	Pomerol
La Fleur-Pomerol	Pomerol
La Gaffelière-Naudes	St Émilion
La Grande-Côte	St Émilion
Lagrange, Cru	Pomerol
Lamarzelle Figeac	St Émilion
La Pointe	Pomerol
Laroze	St Émilion
La Serre	St Émilion
La Tour Figeac	St Émilion
La Tour-Pomerol	Pomerol
Le Cadet	St Émilion
Le Gay	Pomerol
L'Évangile	Pomerol
Magdelaine	St Émilion

Château or Estate	*Commune or Parish*
Nénin	Pomerol
Pavie	St Émilion
Pavie–Decesse	St Émilion
Pavie–Macquin, Domaine de	St Émilion
Pavillon–Cadet	St Émilion
Pelletan	St Émilion
Petit-Faurie-de-Soutard	St Émilion
Petit-Village	Pomerol
Pétrus	Pomerol
Quentin	St Émilion
Saint-Georges-Côte-Pavie	St Émilion
Sansonnet	St Émilion
Soutard	St Émilion
Tertre-Daugay	St Émilion
Trois-Moulins, Les	St Émilion
Troplong-Mondot	St Émilion
Trotanoy	Pomerol
Trottevieille	St Émilion
Vieux-Château-Certan	Pomerol
Villemaurine	St Émilion
Yon-Figeac	St Émilion

Besides the immense quantities of very good Clarets made every year from the vineyards of the Médoc, Graves, and St Émilion districts, there is much wine made in other parts of the Gironde department, some upon the hills between both rivers Dordogne and Garonne, a district known as *Entre-Deux-Mers*, and along the banks of those two rivers as well as near the banks of the Gironde and in the islands of the Gironde, all such low-lying lands being generally known as *palus*.

There is an almost infinite range of Clarets of various degrees of excellence and at different prices, but whether Clarets be young or old, from one of the most famous châteaux or from quite a humble and nameless vineyard, Claret is the most welcome of wines. It does not mean that Claret is the best wine for all people and all occasions; it does not mean that it is bound to appeal to everybody. It means that it is so well balanced – that is to say, that the proportions of its alcohol, acids and ethers are so harmonious that it has the most gentle and beneficial action upon the whole internal economy of most normal people, more particularly upon the nervous system and the digestive organs. This is why Claret never palls, even when drunk daily, and that is also why all the doctors who have taken the trouble to study the chemistry of wine and its dietetic value, have always placed Claret as the most wholesome of all wines.

(b) The Red Wines of Burgundy

Burgundy, like Bordeaux, has always been in France, but, also like Bordeaux, it has not alway been French.

When the Roman Empire finally broke up, Franks, Vandals and Huns swarmed over the Rhine, practically unopposed. The Franks conquered the romanized Gauls along the valleys of the Marne, the Seine, the Loire, and their many tributaries; they pushed back the original Celts into the fastnesses of Brittany and succeeded after much hard fighting in keeping the Norsemen or Normans in Normandy. The Vandals did not fare so well; they followed the valleys of the Moselle, the Doubs, and the Saône, but their progress was checked south of Lyon by the better-armed and more disciplined Gallo-Roman troops; it was checked towards the west by the Massif Central, the great rocky wall of Auvergne. One of the Vandal tribes, the Burgundii, settled in the fifth century in the country west of the Moselle, south of the Marne, east of Auvergne and north of the Rhône, and these have been ever since the extreme limits within which there has been, in turns, a kingdom, a dukedom, and a province of Burgundy, quite distinct from, and often at war with, the Kingdom of France, previous to the year 1477, when Burgundy was finally conquered by the king of France. At the time of the French Revolution, in 1879, the old provinces of France were cut up into smaller departments; two of them, the Côte d'Or, the Saône-et-Loire, as well as part of a third, the Rhône, were carved out of the former province of Burgundy. They are the only departments the wines of which are entitled to be sold under the name of Bourgogne, according to the laws of France, which, of course, are not binding outside France.

The vine was introduced along the valley of the Saône at an early date, and it must be recorded to the credit of the Burgundii that when they invaded the land to which they were to give their name, they behaved in a much more intelligent manner than the Franks did further north; they did not massacre the natives but made them work; they encouraged agriculture in general and viticulture in particular. As early as the seventh century St Gregory of Tours praised the excellence of the wines made from the vineyards of the Dijon hills, but the greatest victory which the red wines of Burgundy gained over all other red wines made in France was when Louis XIV, acting upon the professional advice of his doctor, drank nought but red Burgundy every day. The Grand Monarque thought so well of the red wines of Burgundy that he sent some to Charles II in London, to the King of Poland, and to the Shah of Persia.

Just as Claret had become popular in England during the long time when Bordeaux and its vineyards were under English rule, so the wines of Burgundy became very popular in Flanders during the long spell of Burgundian overlordship. They never reached Paris in any large quantities, owing to the great difficulties of transport, at a time when each province of France had its own frontiers, its own laws and regulations, rates and taxes, and no goodwill whatsoever towards one another. What little Burgundy wine reached England in olden times had to be carted to the Yonne river, sent by barge to the Seine and to Rouen, via Paris, a long voyage and a perilous one in the care of thirsty and not too scrupulous bargees.

The red wines of Burgundy are made from the vineyards of the two departments of Côte d'Or and Saône-et-Loire and those of the northern half of the Rhône department. The Côte d'Or owes its name to a sequence of hills, some thirty-six miles in length, which have proved an inexhaustible gold mine for centuries past, their rugged soil, mostly decomposed granite, producing some of the greatest and most expensive red wines in the world. The hills of the Côte d'Or run from Dijon to

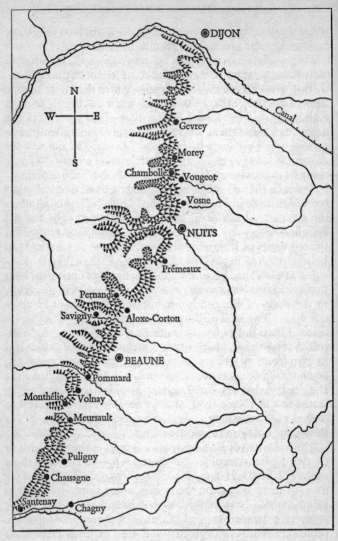

The Vineyards of the Côte d'Or

Chalon-sur-Saône, in a south-south-west direction, and two other ranges of low hills carry more vineyards further south, almost as far south as Lyon, right across the department of Saône-et-Loire and well into that of the Rhône. Those hills are known as the Côte Chalonnaise, the Côte Mâconnaise, and the Hills of the Beaujolais. Their vineyards are responsible for most of the red wines of Burgundy, not the finest of all, but exceedingly pleasant red wines, which are ready for drinking when merely two or three years old. Being made in considerable quantities and fit to drink at an early age, they are or ought to be quite inexpensive.

The wines of the Côte d'Or, which are by far the best red Burgundies, are also better known and in greater demand. They are sold in the majority of cases under the name of the *commune* or parish where the grapes are grown from which they are made; the name of any particularly favoured vineyard, the best known of its individual *commune*, is often used as well as the name of the *commune*, and sometimes in place of it. Lastly the name of the proprietor of the vineyard or that of the shipper of the wine should also appear on the label as a guarantee of quality. There are no vineyards in the Côte d'Or capable of giving more than a fraction of the quantity of grapes which the owner of a château like Lafite or Latour will gather at the time of the vintage. Vineyards are much smaller in Burgundy than in the Gironde, and even when they are fairly large, like the Clos de Vougeot vineyard, the largest by far of the Côte d'Or, they are split up into a number of small holdings – fifty-four different proprietors, for instance, sharing the 125 acres of the Clos de Vougeot. Obviously not all the owners of a share of the same vineyard have the same means, skill, or standards, but they all have the right to sell their wine under the same name, and the consequence is that two or three red Burgundies which bear the name of the same vineyard, but not that of the same owner, may be quite different, the better man's wine being better than that of his more grasping or less painstaking neighbour. Among the finest red Burgundies, besides those of Vougeot, are those from the smallest vineyards, they being most reliable as they are owned by one or at the most two individuals of firms: such are the vineyards of *La Romanée Conti* ($4\frac{1}{2}$ acres), *Richebourg* (12 acres), *La Tâche* ($3\frac{1}{2}$ acres), and *La Romanée* (2 acres), all of them within the bounds of the *commune* of Vosne-Romanée. First place has often been claimed by and given to the red wines of *Chambertin* (32 acres), and those of its twin vineyard *Clos de Bèze* (37 acres), in the *commune* of Gevrey, which now hyphenates its name with that of its best vineyard and is called Gevrey-Chambertin. In the adjoining *commune* of Morey-Saint-Denis, *Les Lambrays* ($22\frac{1}{2}$ acres), and *Clos de Tart* (17 acres) are responsible for some exceedingly fine red wines. Equally fine wines are made from *Le Musigny* (14 acres), *Les Petits Musigny* (10 acres), and also *Les Bonnes Mares*, *Les Amoureuses*, and *Les Charmes*, in the *commune* of Chambolle-Musigny. One of the finest red wines of Burgundy is that made from the best vineyard of the *commune* of Flagey known as *Les Grands Echézeaux*, a name which is a handicap in overseas markets. Last, but by no means least, the red wines of the *commune* of Nuits-Saint-Georges are among the best, more particularly those from the vineyards of *Le Saint-Georges* (18 acres) and *Les Vaucrains* (14 acres).

All these, the finest of all red Burgundies, with but rare exceptions, are those of vineyards planted half-way up the slopes of the low range of hills south of Dijon and north of Beaune, called the *Côte de Nuits*, as distinct from the *Côte de Beaune*, which includes all vineyards from those of Aloxe-Corton, in the north, to those of Santenay, the southern boundary of the Côte d'Or department. The Côte de Beaune vineyards produce a greater quantity of red wines than those of the Côte de Nuits, but only few of them reach, with age, the same high degree of excellence as the best red wines of the Côte de Nuits are capable of attaining.

The two best-known red Burgundy wines, however, are those of Beaune and Pommard, both Côte de Beaune wines, but the fact that these two names are easily pronounced and remembered has led to much abuse. Untold quantities of red wine of doubtful origin have been sold under the names of

Pommard and Beaune, without those names being supported on the bottle's label by the name of any individual vineyard or that of a respectable vintner or shipper.

The other *communes* of the Côte de Beaune which are responsible for the production of much fine red wine are those of Aloxe-Corton, Savigny, Volnay, Monthélie, Auxey, Meursault, Puligny, Chassagne and Santenay. It must be borne in mind that, as in the case of other wine-producing *communes*, their best wines are always offered with the indication of their true parentage, the name of the particular vineyard in their *commune* of origin.

In the case of Aloxe-Corton, for instance, the best vineyards are those of *Corton* (27 acres), *Clos du Roi* (25 acres), and *Les Renardes* (35 acres). The best vineyard of Savigny is *Les Vergelesses;* one of the best of Beaune is *Les Grèves* (79½ acres). By a curious accident of soil formation, some of the red wines of the *commune* of Chassagne, particularly *Le Clos Saint Jean*, are the only ones of the Côte de Beaune which can rival the best of the Côte de Nuits wines, acquiring with bottle age an elegance or charm which is the hall-mark of the Côte de Nuits wines.

For the purpose of reference an alphabetical list of the principal wine-producing *communes* of the Côte d'Or is given here, together with a list of some of their vineyards, in alphabetical order: the *têtes de cuvée* or best wines of each *commune* are in italics.

Parishes	*Vineyards*
ALOXE-CORTON.	Bressandes; *Charlemagne; Clos du Roi; Les Chaumes; Le Corton;* Les Grèves; Les Meix; Les Perrières; *Les Renardes;* La Vigne au Saint.
BEAUNE.	Les Aigrots; Blanche Fleur; *Bressandes;* Les Cent Vignes; *Champimonts;* Le Choicheux; *Le Clos de la Mousse; Le Clos des Mouches;* Le Clos du Roi; *Aux Cras;* Les Épenottes; *Les Fèves; Les Grèves; Les Marconnets;* La Mign-

Parishes	Vineyards
	otte; En l'Orme; Les Perrières; Pertuisots; Les Seurey; Les Sizies; Les Theurons; Tiélandry; Les Toussaints; Les Vignes Franches.
CHAMBOLLE-MUSIGNY.	Les Amoureuses; Les Baudes; *Les Bonnes Mares;* Les Charmes; Le Combe d'Orveau; Les Cras; Derrière la Grange; Les Fuées; Les Lavrottes; *Le Musigny; Les Petits Musigny;* Les Sentiers.
CHASSAGNE-MONTRACHET.	Le Bâtard-Montrachet; *La Boudriotte;* Les Brussonnes; Les Chaumées; *Clos Saint Jean;* La Maltroie; *Le Montrachet;* Les Morgeots.
FIXIN.	Les Arvelets; Aux Cheusots; Clos du Chapitre; Les Hervelets; Les Meix-Bas; *La Pierrière.*
FLAGEY-ECHÉZEAUX.	Les Beaux-Monts-Bas; Champs-Traversins; Clos St Denis; *Echézeaux du Dessus; Les Grands Echézeaux;* En Orveaux; Les Poulaillères.
GEVREY-CHAMBERTIN.	Cazetiers; *Chambertin;* Chapelle–Chambertin; Charmes–Chambertin; *Clos de Bèze;* Clos Saint Jacques; Griotte–Chambertin; Latricières–Chambertin; Maziz-Chambertin; Mazoyères-Chambertin; Ruchottes-Chambertin; Varoilles.
MEURSAULT.	Les Caillerets; Les Charmes; Les Cras; Les Genevrières; La Goutte d'Or; Les Pelures; *Les Perrières.*
MONTHÉLIE.	Les Cras Rougeot; Les Champs Fulliot; Le Château Gaillard; Le Clos Gauthey.
MOREY-SAINT-DENIS.	*Les Bonnes Mares;* Les Bouchots; Aux Charmes; *Clos de la Roche; Clos de Tart; Clos Saint Denis; Clos des Lambrays.*

Parishes	Vineyards
NUITS-SAINT-GEORGES.	*Les Boudots; Les Cailles;* Le Chaboeufs; Chagnots; *Aux Cras; Aux Murgers;* La Perrière; *Les Porrets;* Les Poulettes; Les Procès; *Les Pruliers;* La Richemone; Roncière; *Le Saint-Georges; Les Vaucrains.*
PERNAND-VERGELESSES.	Les Basses Vergelesses; Les Fichots; *Île des Vergelesses.*
POMMARD.	Les Argillières; Les Arvelets; Les Bertins; Les Boucherottes; Les Charmots; *Le Clos Blanc*; Les Combes Dessus; Les Croix Noires; *Les Épenots;* Les Fremiers; Les Jarollières; Les Pézerolles; Les Poutures; *Les Rugiens Bas;* Les Rugiens Hauts; Les Sausilles; Village de Pommard.
PRÉMEAUX.	Les Argillières; Clos Arlots; Clos des Fourches; *Les Corvées; Les Didiers; Les Forets;* Aux Perdrix.
PULIGNY-MONTRACHET.	Le Bâtard – Montrachet; Blagny-Blanc; Les Chalumeaux; Champ-Canet; Les Combettes; La Garenne; Hameau de Glagny; *Montrachet;* Les Pucelles.
SANTENAY.	*Les Gravières.*
SAVIGNY.	Aus Gravains; *Les Jarrons;* Les Marconnets; *Les Vergelesses.*
VOLNAY.	*Les Angles; Les Caillerets;* Caillerets Dessus; *En Champans;* En Chevret; *Frémiets;* Les Mitans.
VOSNE-ROMANÉE.	Les Beaux-Monts; Aux Brûlées; Grande Rue; Les Malconsorts; *Les Richebourg; La Romanée; La Romanée Conti;* La Romanée Saint-Vivant; *La Tâche.*
VOUGEOT.	*Clos de Vougeot;* Les Petits-Vougeots; La Vigne Blanche.

The fine red wines of the Côte d'Or have, as a rule, a greater volume of bouquet and a higher alcoholic strength than the majority of fine red wines of Bordeaux; they are, on the whole, more distinctive and more assertive, and they owe their excellence not only to the nature of the soil of their vineyards and to the suitable climate of that part of France, but also to the fact that they are made exclusively from Pinot Noir grapes. The Pinot is an aristocrat among vines; it is fastidious as regards soil and aspect, and it is what is called a shy bearer, the fruit which it bears not being either large or plentiful. But the vintner who overlooks all such failings and is content to have fewer bunches of Pinot grapes rather than a lot of Gamay or any other common sort, will be rewarded by making a much finer wine, a wine which will be worth keeping so that it may, in time, show the breed of its noble parentage. Needless to say, not all Burgundy vintners are content to grow Pinot grapes and make fine wine; there is also much wine made in Burgundy from the commoner Gamay grapes, some of it made even in the Côte d'Or department, but most of it in the Saône-et-Loire and Rhône departments, further south. Such wines are by no means to be despised, but they ought not to be binned away and left to mature in dark, deep cellars. They can be, and they often are, very pleasant indeed, when young, and the fact that they are of more common parentage than the famous growths of the Côte d'Or is no blemish on this our age, the age of the common man.

The best wines of the Saône-et-Loire department are those of the Côte Chalonnaise, a range of hills facing the right bank of the river Saône, from Chagny to Tournus, where the Pinot grape is still extensively grown for the making of the better types of red wines.

The best-known wine of the Côte Chalonnaise is that of Mercurey, a red wine which is not of uniform quality since there are no less that 1,750 acres planted in vines, most of them Pinot, but some others Gamay, producing the wine which is entitled to the name of *Mercurey*.

To the south of the Côte Chalonnaise, other hills, also facing the right bank of the river Saône, are known as the Côte Mâcon-

naise, or *Le Mâconnais*, beginning south of Tournus and ending
at Romanèche-Thorins. It is only at the southern limit of the
Côte Mâconnaise, which is also the southern limit of the Saône-
et-Loire, that they make red wines of some distinction, the best
of them being the wines of *Moulin-à-Vent*, from the vineyards
of two adjoining *communes*, Romanèche-Thorins, in Saône-et-
Loire, and Chenas, in the Rhône.

Further south still, in the department of Rhône, as far as
Villefranche, the hills of the Beaujolais are covered with vines,
Gamay vines, and they produce an abundance of red wines
which are classed as red Burgundies, wines of lighter texture
than those made from Pinot grapes further north, but nevertheless quite attractive wines and attractively inexpensive as
well. The more popular red wines of the Beaujolais are those
from the vineyards of Brouilly, Chiroubles, Fleurie, Juliénas,
Saint Amour and Morgan.

The lot of the Burgundy shipper is, indeed, a most difficult
one. He has to deal with a large number of small vineyards each
one of which produces too small a quantity of wine for the
ordinary commercial needs of any firm with a worldwide connection. The only thing for him to do is to blend them together,
like the Champagne shippers do, who are also faced with a
similar problem of many small vineyards to deal with. The
difference is that the many wines of the Champagne vineyards
have everything to gain and nothing to lose – bar their own
name – through being blended together in an intelligent
manner. Moreover, the Champagne shipper, that is the man
who is responsible for the more or less intelligent – hence
successful – blending of those different wines, offers them to the
world, not under the name of Ay or Verzenay or any particular
vineyard, but under his own name and responsibility. The
Burgundy shipper never owned up to his blends in a sufficiently
bold spirit to offer them under his own name or mark. For
generations he sold them under the name of one or other of the
vineyards or parishes of the Côte d'Or, names such as Pommard, Beaune, or Vougeot, names which have by now sunk

deep into the minds of all sorts of people all over the world. In this way a few names of the Burgundy country have acquired a far greater measure of popularity than the limited quantity of their own wines would have entitled them to.

All might have been well had not some of the Burgundy shippers overstepped the mark in the matter of blending. Blending is to some extent like kissing – it may be quite innocent, but it may lead one away from the narrow path of duty and propriety. When the demand was good and the supply poor the temptation was great for some of the more progressive shippers of Burgundy to blend with a little true Burgundy wine a great deal of some other wine from the South of France or Algeria, much to the hurt of the fair name of the wines of the Côte d'Or and greatly to the detriment of the painstaking small owners who tried hard to grow the best grapes and to make the best wine possible. They complained, and the public complained, too. The law stepped in. It was high time that the law should step in when it did. But the law has a very clumsy way of stepping in; it means well but it is flat-footed. No wine of Burgundy may now be sold under any other name than its own. It sounds grand. It is quite all right for the growers whose vineyards happen to be in the parishes of Beaune, Volnay, Vougeot, Pommard, Corton, and a few more, the names of which are both known abroad and easier of pronunciation. But it is not nearly so good an arrangement for the unfortunate *vignerons* of parishes which do not happen to be known beyond their own province, or are too difficult for any but Frenchmen to pronounce properly. Who, for instance, ever heard of Auxey-Duresses, Brochon, Fixen, Flagey-Echézeaux, Pernand-Vergelesses, Prémeaux, Prissey, or Serrigny? And yet they all, and a number of others, produce some very good Pinot-made Burgundies which reached the public, in other days, under the better-known names of some neighbouring parish. But now the wines of Auxey-Duresses, for instance, can no longer be sold as wines of Monthélie, as in the past, nor the wines of Monthélie-cum-Auxey be sold under the better-known name of Volnay. If they are offered to the public under their totally unknown name of Auxey-Duresses, the public, always shy of newcomers, will have none of it. What is to be done?

The only answer which the Burgundy shippers have so far found has been the creation of marks of their own. They came to the conclusion that it would be quite as difficult to create a demand among the public for names of parishes or of vineyards hitherto unknown as to create a demand for absolutely fictitious names registered by each one of them as their own brands. Moreover, were they to spend money to make the name of Auxey-Duresses popular, the small yield of wines from that particular parish might very well become exhausted in a very short time, and the demand created among the public would have to be met by apologies and the 'All Gone' signal. On the contrary, if they, the shippers, were to spend money in order to make popular the *Château Blue Goose* or *Clos Sunkist*, they could sell under those registered names the whole of the wines of Auxey-Duresses and follow them up with any other wines blended or mended in such a way as to give satisfaction to the buyers thereof.

HOSPICES DE BEAUNE   Nicolas Rolin and his wife Guigone de Salins founded a home for the poor and aged at Beaune, in 1443, and by way of endowment each bequeathed to this home, or *Hospices de Beaune*, a vineyard. In the course of time other vineyards were bequeathed to the *hospices*, and the wines made from those vineyards are sold every year for its upkeep. These are the genuine Hospices de Beaune wines. There are twenty-nine such *cuvées*, or wines from vineyards belonging to the Hospices, twenty-two *cuvées* of red wines and seven of white wines. Nine of the red wine *cuvées* are from Beaune vineyards, four from Savigny, two each from Meursault, Aloxe-Corton, Pommard and Volnay, and one each from Auxey and Monthélie. Hence the *Hospices de Beaune* wines are far from being of uniform quality or standard and they are always sold under the name of one or the other of the twenty-two individual *cuvées*, the list of which is here appended for reference:

T–C

Cuvée	Vineyards
Nicolas Rolin	Beaune
Guigone de Salins	Beaune
Clos des Avaux	Beaune
Brunet	Beaune
Pierre Virely	Beaune
Bétault	Beaune
Rousseau Deslandes	Beaune
Dames Hospitalières	Beaune
Estienne	Beaune
Fouquerand	Savigny
Arthur Girard	Savigny
Du Bay-Peste	Savigny
Forneret	Savigny
Jehan de Massol	Meursault
Gauvain	Meursault
Docteur Peste	Aloxe-Corton
Charlotte Dumay	Aloxe-Corton
Boillot	Auxey
Dames de la Charité	Pommard
Billardet	Pommard
Jacques Lebelin	Monthélie
Blondeau	Volnay
Général Muteau	Volnay

(c) Other European Red Beverage Wines

ASSMANSHAUSEN   The vineyards which rise steeply from the sprawling little town of Assmanshausen, on the right bank of the Rhine, in the Rheingau, produce one of the few red beverage wines of the Rhine which have acquired a measure of reputation outside their native village. The best vineyards of Assmanshausen are those of Hinterkirch, Frankental, and Höllenberg.

BAROLO   One of the best red wines of Italy. It is made from the vineyards of a strictly delimited district of Piedmont known as *Le Langhe*, which includes, besides the parish of *Barolo*, those of *Castiglion Faletto*, *La Morra*, *Monfirte*, *Verduno*,

Perno, Serralunga, and *Grinzone*. The little village of Barolo, which gives its name to the wines of the surrounding vineyards, is perched upon the top of an extinct volcano, upon the slopes of which the Nebbiolo grape grows to perfection and produces a truly excellent red wine, deep in colour, fairly high in alcoholic strength, and not deficient in bouquet like practically all other red beverage wines of Italy.

There is another red wine made in the same and surrounding districts from the same grapes as the Barolo, but it is distinctly inferior to it: it is usually sold as Bardolino. A more inferior red wine is made in many parts of northern Italy; it is sold under the name of Barbera, but it is not bought by the *cognoscenti*.

CHÂTEAUNEUF-DU-PAPE   One of the best beverage red wines of the Rhône Valley, in the Vaucluse department, a little south of Orange. The wines of Châteauneuf-du-Pape are made from a number of different species of grapes, and whether this blending of grapes or the nature of the soil of the vineyards be the cause of it – probably they each have a share of responsibility – the fact is that the red wines of Châteauneuf-du-Pape possess remarkable tonic properties. They diffuse a heat within and ensure a lasting glow which is a gift entirely their own, and one which is not due to any greater alcoholic strength than other red wines. Some of them are inclined to be a little brutal, but only a little, and only when the vintage of their birth was not of the best.

There are a number of different châteaux or estates at Châteauneuf-du-Pape, the names of which appear on the labels of the bottles as a guarantee of authenticity and reliability. Such are the Châteaux de la Nerthe, Nallys, Saint Patrice, Fortia, and Clos des Papes.

CHIANTI   The best known of the red beverage wines of Italy, and the best, after the wine of Barolo. Chianti is made mostly from the vineyards of the three parishes of Radda, Castellina, and Gaiole, a district known as Chianti Ferresse, in the province of Siena in Tuscany. The red wines made from vineyards in the adjoining parishes of Castelnuovo, Bererdegna, the Terzo de Siena, and a few others, are also entitled to be sold under the name of Chianti.

Chianti is made from a number of different sorts of grapes, and as it is made in enormous quantities there are wide differences in quality, or the lack thereof, between one straw-covered flask of Chianti and another. The most reliable brand of Chianti is that of Barone Ricasoli, the largest vineyard owner in Tuscany, whose wines are sold under the registered name of Brolio Chianti.

Owing to the fact that it is bottled in flasks which are difficult to cork securely and impossible to bin away properly, Chianti is drunk while young and somewhat tart. Its hardness and acidity make it an excellent thirst-quencher, and it is also acceptable with oily or highly spiced food; it is also claimed for Chianti that it helps digestion and prevents constipation, but it is not claimed to rival the red wines of Bordeaux or Burgundy.

The much higher standard of excellence of Chianti is due to progress made under the Consorzio per la Difesa del Vino Tipico del Chianti responsible for the Chianti Classico marketed under the black cockerel on gold background seal.

COLARES The ruby wines of Colares have enjoyed a considerable reputation for a great deal longer than any of the other table wines of Portugal. They are made from Ramisco grapes grown on sandy soil in the lower valley of the Tagus.

CORTAILLOD The best red wine made in Switzerland, from some of the Canton of Neuchâtel vineyards. It has the colour and attractive bouquet of one of the lesser but good red Burgundies, and it is made from a variety of the Burgundian Pinot grape.

CÔTES DU RHÔNE This is a name which might be claimed by any and every of the many wines made here and there, practically everywhere along one or the other or both banks of the river Rhône, from Switzerland to the Mediterranean, but as a matter of commercial practice the name is restricted to the wines made from grapes grown in the Rhône valley between Lyon and Avignon, a stretch which includes the vineyards of Côte Rôtie, Hermitage and Châteauneuf-du-Pape, the three finest Côtes du Rhône wines. The red wines which are sold under the name of Côtes du Rhône, always in Burgundy-shaped bottles, may be expected to be deep red in colour, rather heady, a little coarse, comforting, but not really fine: were they really fine they would have a name of their own.

CÔTE RÔTIE   The red wines of Côte Rôtie of a good vintage are very fine wines and easily the finest of the Rhône wines, provided, of course, that they be given time to mature and show their worth. They are made from the vineyards of the *commune* of Ampuis, south of Lyon, near the ancient Roman city of Vienne, but the quantity available is so small that they are very difficult to buy.

DAO   The red wines of the Dao region, in the southern half of the Beira Alta Province, are now available in the British Isles at prices which are particularly attractive. They are made mostly from the Tourigo and Preto Mortagua grapes grown in terraced vineyards at quite high altitudes in the valleys of both the rivers Dao and Mondego.

EGRI BIKAVER   The darkest and one of the best red wines of Hungary, from the vineyards of the Eger district. It is a fairly strong wine, a quality which its name is intended to convey, *Bikaver* meaning *Bull's Blood*. A more delicate table wine made in the same district of Eger is called *Egri Kadarka*.

HERMITAGE   The name of a small hill which rises fairly steeply from the little town of Tain, on the left bank of the Rhône, opposite the larger town of Tournon; also the name of the wines made from the vineyards which are planted mostly half-way up the hill, a few of them near the top, where, in olden times, there used to be a small chapel and there used to live a holy hermit. The wines of Hermitage enjoyed a high degree of fame until the phylloxera destroyed all the vineyards, towards the close of the last century. They have been replanted since, but their wines have not yet quite recaptured the position which pre-phylloxera Hermitage held in the estimation of wine connoisseurs.

The best red wines of Hermitage are those from the vineyards known as La Chapelle, Les Baissards, and Rochefine.

RETSINA The name which is usually given to the majority of the Greek table wines, a resinated wine which is an acquired taste; the Greeks appear to have acquired it.

RIOJA The vineyards which produce the Rioja wines are separated by the river Ebro into Rioja and Rioja Alta. The centre of the Rioja wine trade is the town of Haro, while Logroño is the centre of Rioja Alta vineyards. There are a number of quite different red wines entitled to the name Rioja, some made from Cabernet grapes, which are called *Burdeos*, in Spain; others from the Graciano, Tempranillo, Garnachio and some commoner grapes, hence the importance of the shipper's name as a guarantee of fine quality. Among the best Rioja wines shippers are the Marqués de Riscal, the Bodegas Bilbainas, La Vinicola del Norte de España, Marqués de Murrieta, and Gomez Cruzado.

ROMANIA Between the wars, from 1919 to 1939, Romania ranked fourth in order of importance among the great wine-producing countries of Europe, after France, Italy, and Spain. It is not possible to know what present conditions are and all that one can say is that the best wines of Romania were the following, at a time when the regions mentioned were within the borders of Romania: Akkerman, in Bessarabia; Cotnari, in the province of Moldau; Dealul Marc in the province of Muntenia; Dragashani, in the province of Oltenia;

Sarica, Constanza, Silistria, and Turtucaia, in Dobrudscha;
Alba Julia, Tarnaval, Arad, Bihorteleagd, Satul Marc, and
Halmei, in the Siebenbürgen district.

TOURAINE The red wines of Touraine are produced by
the same species of grapes as those of the Médoc, chiefly the
Cabernet, which is known in Touraine as the Breton grape; it
has nothing to do with Brittany, but was introduced by an
Abbé Breton in the seventeenth century. Long before that,
they made *le vin clairet et vermeil frais* in Rabelais's country, fair
Touraine, and the same type of red wine is still being made
from the vineyards of Chinon, near Rabelais's birthplace, Joué
and Bourgueil, to name but three of the better-known red
wines of Touraine. And it is still the practice to serve the red
wines of Touraine at cellar's temperature, as recommended by
Rabelais of old.

VOSLAUER The best known and one of the best red table
wines of Austria. It is a very dark red wine, made mostly from
the common Blue Portugieser grapes.

II. WHITE BEVERAGE WINES

Red wines are red, but white wines are not white, they are
yellow; they may be called golden or amber, which sounds
better than yellow, but they never are quite white. However,
whatever their colour, all wines made from white grapes are
by common consent called white wines. Most white beverage
wines are made in the same manner as the red – that is to say, the
grapes are picked when ripe and pressed, their sweet juice runs
out and ferments, thus becoming wine. As a matter of general
rule, it may be said that the sweeter and riper the grapes, the
darker will be the gold or amber of white wines. In the valley
of the Moselle, for instance, white wines are much paler than
those made in the valley of the Garonne or in that of the Douro.
That is, of course, provided they are not artificially coloured or
discoloured. There are people who are not satisfied with the

pale looks of their white wines: they give them a darker tint by adding burnt sugar, or caramel, which makes them look richer. There are others whose wines, made in the sun-drenched vinelands, possess a deeper shade of amber than happens to be popular locally, and they are foolish enough to bleach their wines with chemicals in order to make them look like the white beverage wines of more northern latitudes. There are even worse offenders: there are people who treat red wines chemically in such a way as to make them into white wines, in order to meet the demand for white wines at a time when such wines happen to be in shorter supply and fetching higher prices. This practice is wrong even if it happens to be legal, and the wines so treated are never worth buying, and still less worth drinking. But there are also some white wines which are made from black grapes in what may be called a perfectly legitimate way. In practically all the European species of grapes the juice is white and the colouring red pigment is in the lining of the skins of black grapes. When black grapes are pressed, their white juice becomes dyed red after it has been fermenting in contact with the black skins in the fermenting vat. If pressed in such a way that the juice is run at once into a separate vat or tub where it is left to ferment away from the skins that are held back in the press, white wine will result, a white wine free from all interference with objectionable chemicals, which ruin all bleached wines.

The white beverage wines of the world may be divided into two main classes, the dry and the sweet. The dry white wines are made from those grapes which contain no more natural sugar than can be transformed by fermentation into alcohol and carbonic acid gas, whereas sweet white wines are made from grapes which contain more sugar than can be disposed of by natural fermentation. This happens when white grapes, instead of being gathered as soon as they reach their optimum degree of ripeness, are allowed to remain unpicked until they have lost some of their water content so that the proportion of sugar to water in each berry is increased appreciably. When such grapes are pressed there is less of their juice available, but the loss is entirely a loss of water, all the sugar is still there, and more of it than fermentation is able to deal with, so that the wine which is eventually obtained is sweet to the taste.

The best and best-known dry white wines are those of the Moselle, Rhine, Alsace, Burgundy, Chablis and Graves vineyards, while the best-known naturally sweet wines – naturally sweet as distinct from sweetened wines – are those of Sauternes, Anjou, and the Palatinate.

White wines, like all natural wines, are liable to cast off, as they age in cask or bottle, a sediment which, in their case, is all the more undesirable in that it is more immediately apparent and spoils the look of the wine. There was a time when a little sediment in a white wine was generally accepted as proof of the wine being natural, but wine drinkers have become more fastidious, even if less knowledgeable, and they reject any white wine in which they can detect bits and pieces floating about when the wine is served. In Victorian days, white wines were usually served in coloured glasses which made such 'bits and pieces' more or less invisible, but coloured glasses are no longer the fashion, and pure white glasses are now *de rigueur*. White glasses are best if one is to enjoy the colour of wine, be it purple or golden, and white wines cannot be expected to be entirely free from all sediment unless they have been matured in cask for a sufficiently long period before they are most carefully racked and bottled; also, when kept in bottle for a long time, if they are fully decanted before being served. Both time and care are, unfortunately, expensive luxuries, and there is a much quicker and cheaper way of making sure that white wine is going to be 'star bright' and remain bright, if not for ever at any rate as long as any white wine is likely to be kept in bottle: it is done by filtering. Modern filters are most efficient; they retain the minutest particles of free matter in suspension in a wine, and the filtered white wine is and remains quite bright, but it has also been robbed of minute yet by no means unimportant elements which it could ill afford to lose: it is brighter but not better.

(a) Moselle and Rhine

MOSELLE WINES The Moselle is one of the most beautiful rivers of Europe; it is also one of the most twisty. It rises in the east of France, spends the greater part of its course meandering through French valleys and vineyards, all the time making for the North Sea as best it can. Then it appears to give up the attempt and to decide that it had better get there on the back, or rather in the bed, of old Father Rhine. It takes a sharp turn towards the east, cuts across Luxembourg to Germany, and at last meets the Rhine at Koblenz. There it ends as a river and becomes just part of the Rhine.

Vines grow and wine is made practically all along the course of the Moselle, but none of more than local fame until the Moselle has passed Trier. It is during the last lap of the Moselle's chequered course, from Trier to Koblenz, that we find the vineyards which produce the finest wines, the only wines with a world-wide reputation, white wines which in good years combine the most exquisite, light, gossamer-like charm with real breed and true aristocratic character.

The run of the Moselle from Trier to Koblenz is lovely and far from smooth. The river works and worms its way, like a snake that smells a mongoose coming, through a chaotic mass of hills steep enough to have had most of their soil washed down in the course of ages, leaving bare slabs of rock exposed to the view of the passer-by, who wonders how so many healthy vines manage to hang on and apparently to thrive on such poor, slaty, rocky ground. Of course they couldn't were it not for the picturesque little villages all along the river banks, villages with solid houses, wherein live solid, hard-working folks, while outside for all who pass by to see and envy, stands and stinks a solid pile of well-seasoned manure. Farm manure is nature's own milk for those vines planted in the schistous rock; it is incomparably better than all the patent chemical fertilizers. The vines of the Moselle's best vineyards have, indeed, their full share of this life's difficulties. They have hardly any soil for their roots and the most trying weather conditions to ripen their

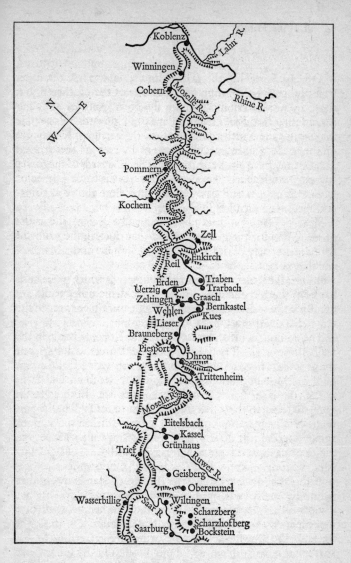

The Moselle Vineyards

grapes. They live for ever in fear of frosts. Very hard frosts they stand extraordinarily well, during the winter, but the late frosts, the spring frosts, nip the flowers in the bud. They often get frosts again in the autumn before the grapes are gathered, but those are not so serious as the spring frosts. Another gnawing care of theirs is the fear that they may not get enough sunshine during the summer months to ripen their grapes. If they get one year of golden sunshine grapes to two of sun-starved grapes, they have done rather well. The vineyards of the lower Moselle would have disappeared but for the saving grace of having as masters and slaves at the same time the most pains-taking race of men left in the world. Farm manure is all very well in its place – and its place is not in the sun, but in the ground; and for the grapes to grow and ripen in the valley of the Moselle, they must have also good, honest, human sweat – and they get it.

Besides the wines made from the vineyards which grace both banks of the Moselle, from Trier to Koblenz, other wines are usually known abroad as Moselle Wines, having very much the same characteristics – light greenish colour, delicacy, finesse, and more bouquet than body. They are the wines made in the valleys of two small rivers, the Saar and Ruwer, tributaries of the Moselle. The Saar, which runs in a north-westerly direction, joins the Moselle a few miles above Trier. Its finest vineyards are on the right bank, from Saarburg to the south as far as Euchariusberg to the north. Near Saarburg is Ockfen, the best wine of which is Bockstein, and a little further the famous Scharzhofberg, the finest growth of the Saar valley. Other fine wines of the Saar are the Scharzberger, and those of Agritius-berg, Wiltingen, Kanzem, Wawern, and Oberemmel.

Below the ancient city of Trier the Moselle is met by another tributary, the Ruwer, with only a few vineyards of note, but those may rightly claim to produce as fine wines as the best vineyards of the Moselle proper, if not better. On the right bank of the Ruwer, the best vineyard is an old Carthusian one known as Karthäushofberg, at Eitelsbach. On the other bank the finest wine is the Maximin Grünhäuser. There are also some delicious wines made from the vineyards of Kassel on the right bank of the Ruwer.

From the Ruwer down the Moselle to Koblenz by boat is a delightful trip, if one has time, an eye for beauty, and a sufficient supply of Moselle wine on board. Upon the right bank of the Moselle one passes by Leiwen, Neumagen, Dhron, Filzen, Mulheim, before coming to the famous Bernkastel, where one should break the journey and replenish the ship's store. There are many vineyards upon the steep slopes overlooking Bernkastel by the Moselle; Kirchengrube, Pfaffenberg, Rosenberg, Badstube, Graben, etc., but none so famous as the Doktor. The finest vineyards of the right bank of the Moselle begin at Bernkastel, stretching northwards to Graach, the Josefshöfer vineyards, those of Zeltingen, Erden, Trabach, and Enkirch. Further on we come to Zell, Merl, Senheim, and Valwig, all of which can show good wines when the sun is kind to them.

The left bank of the Moselle, from the Ruwer down towards Koblenz, has almost as many vines as the right, beginning with those of Mehring and Trittenheim. Then come Piesport, Kesten, the Brauneberger hills, a very important wine-producing centre, Lieser, Kues, the twin of Bernkastel, with the Moselle and a fine bridge between them; Wehlen, Uerzig, Kinheim, Traben facing Trabach; Reil, Aldegund, Ediger, Pommern, Hatzenport and Winningen.

RHINE WINES OR HOCKS   The wines of the Rhine were known in England, in the olden times, as Rhenish, but they are now known as Hocks, from the wines of Hochheim, or such, at any rate, is the accepted origin of the name. Hocks are grown on deeper soil than Moselles and have more power; they also acquire with age more colour and greater vinosity. There is something in them more satisfying, more complete and replete than in most Moselles. Majesty is their leading suit; Moselles play to Grace.

Abroad, the most celebrated Rhine wines are those of the Rheingau, Rheinhessen, the Palatinate and Franconia.

Rheingau. The Rheingau vineyards are on the right bank of the

Rhine and may be said to begin opposite Bingen, and to end with the hills of Rauenthal. It is within that comparatively small area that the most famous Rheingau vineyards, which yield wines second to none in the world in point of excellence, are found; the wines are eagerly bought, at the vintage, at prices far higher than those given for new wines in any other vine-growing country.

After leaving Rüdesheim, one comes to Geisenheim, Winkel, Mittelheim, and Östrich, near the Rhine, while higher up the hills are the castles of Johannisberg and Vollrads, surrounded by magnificent vineyards. A little further east are the no less celebrated hills of Steinberg, while nearer the river are the famous growths of Hattenheim, Marcobrunn, Erbach, and Eltville.

Rheinhessen. On the opposite bank of the Rhine, in Hessen, there are a far greater number of vineyards from Bingen to Mainz and from Mainz to Worms, than in the Rheingau, but there is only comparatively a small percentage of the wines made in this province which can claim to possess the same high degree of excellence. Some vineyards in Hessen, however, produce very fine wines, with good body and bouquet, which are eminently suited for export. The best of these are the wines of Nierstein and Oppenheim, some miles south of Mainz, and those of Ingelheim, Laubenheim, Bodenheim, and Nackenheim further north.

As regards the tributaries of the Rhine other than the Moselle, the Ahr and the Nahe, on the left, the Lahn, the Main and the Neckar, on the right, are the most important ones. Extensive vineyards are cultivated in the valleys of all these rivers, and they produce both much white wine and some red wine as well. Walporzheim, on the Ahr, and Hochheim, on the Main, are the two most celebrated growths of these tributaries of the Rhine, the first being famous for its red wines, and the second for its white wines.

Palatinate. The Palatinate vineyards differ from all others in the Rhineland, being the only ones which are not grown in sheltered valleys, or on the steep slopes of the hills which border

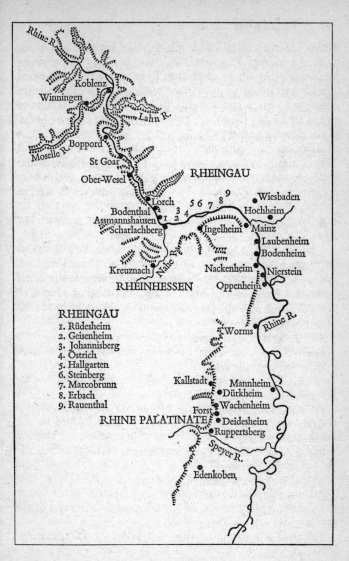

The Rhine Vineyards

the Rhine and its tributaries. They are situated on a plateau, protected from high winds by a mountain range, and they are planted in a soil chiefly of alluvial origin, mostly with southern aspects. The wines made in that district are very distinct from those of the Rheingau, being more luscious but not always so lasting. The first growths of the Palatinate are Deidesheim, Forst, Dürkheim, Wachenheim, Ruppertsberg, Kallstadt, Königsbach, and Neustadt.

Franconia. In Franconia, once part of Bavaria, further east and north, the white Stein wines are very characteristic, and in very good years they are also very fine. They are usually sold in peculiar-shaped bottles known as *Boxbeutel*.

Liebfraumilch is a name used for any Rhine wine of fair quality; it does not come from any one district or vineyard.

A bottle of Hock or Moselle with just a name, be it Bernkastel, Rüdesheim, Nierstein, or any other, may contain good, bad or indifferent wine; the odds are that the wine in the bottle with just a bare name will be *ordinaire*. The label of a Hock or Moselle bottle may also bear all sorts of names which have each a meaning of their own.

Auslese means *specially selected*.

Beerenauslese is one better; it means that the berries of each bunch were specially selected.

Goldbeerenauslese is one better still; only the ripest berries from each bunch were used to make the wine.

Feine and *Feinste* mean *Fine* and *Finest*.

Creszenz means 'the Growth of', and is followed by the name of the grower.

Gewächs means the same as *Creszenz;* 'the property of' instead of 'the growth of'.

Kellerabzug means 'from the cellar of . . .'

Originalabfüllung means 'bottled by the grower'.

Spätlese means 'late vintage', a wine made at the end of the vintage, when the grapes are ripest.

Wachstum means 'the property of', followed by the name of the vineyard owner.

Moselles are usually bottled in blue-green bottles, whereas

Hocks are as a rule bottled in reddish-brown bottles, a difference which is convenient in the binning away and service of these wines.

Moselles are, generally speaking, at their best when quite young, from two to six years, but there are exceptions to all rules and some Moselles, vintaged in particularly fine years, have been shown to improve in bottle for twenty years.

Hocks, as a rule, need longer to show their worth, and some of the wines of the great classical vintages of the past have stood admirably the test of time. Such wines, however, are the exceptions, and the rule is for Hocks, as well as for all beverage white wines, that they have more to lose than to gain by being kept as long as red wines.

One of the distinctive merits of Hocks and Moselles is the greater measure of individuality than most other white wines possess. The wine of one vineyard is not blended with the wine of the next vineyard, or of any other vineyards, in order to average quality and cost, as is done almost everywhere else where white wines are made commercially, but the wine made from the day's picking is, very often, kept to itself and not blended with the wine from the grapes grown in the very same vineyard, but picked the next day or days, when they may have been either better because more fully ripe, or, on the contrary, not quite so perfect, because over-ripe or not so sound. This is why the rotation or identifying number of each cask is usually stated on invoice and label in the case of the finer wines of the best vintages. While this almost excessive care to retain for each cask, almost for each bottle, the fullest measure of individuality is highly to be commended in an age all too prone to vattings, blendings, and mediocrity, it is responsible for the very high cost of all the finest wines of the Rhine and Moselle, more particularly the first. Before the First World War, during the last quarter of the nineteenth century and the first decade of the twentieth, well-to-do Germans did not hesitate to pay £5 per bottle for young wines of fine pedigree and of good vintages. Such wines were made, and must of necessity always be made, in such small quantities that their prices are bound to be out of all proportion to their intrinsic worth whenever there are a number of people eager to secure that which is best, whatever the cost.

There is, however, every reason to expect that in future there will be some Moselles and Hocks blended and made up to certain types more regular as well as more mediocre in quality, and more reasonable in price than in the past.

A list of the principal Wine-Producing Districts of Germany, and of their best Vineyards

OBERMOSEL

Villages	*Districts*	*Best Vineyards*
Nittel	Saarburg	Vogelsberg, Leiterchen, Gipfel.
Wellen	Saarburg	Altenberg, Scharzberg, Steinkaul.

MITTELMOSEL

Bernkastel		Doktor, Schlossberg, Badstube, Pfaffenberg, Rosenberg, Graben, Lay, Altenwald.
Kues	Bernkastel	Weissenstein, Königsstuhl, Herrenberg.
Brauneberg	Bernkastel	Hasenläufer, Falkenberg, Juffer, Bürgerslay, Nonnenlay.
Dhron	Bernkastel	Sängerei, Kandel, Hofberg, Roterd, Dhronhofberger.
Enkirch	Zell	Steffensberg Löwenbaum, Kreuzpfad, Herrenberg, Nonnengarten, Ellergrub, Montaneubel, Klosterberg.
Erden	Bernkastel	Treppchen, Prälat, Herzlei, Pichter, Busslay, Herrenberg.
Graach	Bernkastel	Himmelreich, Domprobst, Abstberg, Müzlay, Goldwingert, Rosenberg, Josefshöfer.
Lieser	Bernkastel	Neiderberg, Pfaffenberg, Paulsberg, Schlossberg, Helden.
Piesport	Wittlich	Goldtröpfchen, Pichter, Falkenberg, Lay, Schubertslay, Taubengarten, Güterslay.

MITTELMOSEL (*cont.*)

Villages	Districts	Best Vineyards
Traben	Zell	Königsberg, Kräuterhaus, Würzgarten.
Trabach	Zell	Burgberg, Schlossberg, Hünerberg.
Trittenheim	Trier	Falkenberg, Laurentiusberg, Olk, Apotheke.
Uerzig	Wittlich	Kranklay, Würzgarten, Schwarzlay.
Wehlen	Bernkastel	Sonnenuhr, Lay, Klosterberg, Nonnenberg, Feinter.
Zell		Schwarze Katz.
Zeltingen	Bernkastel	Kirchenpfad, Stefanslay, Steinmauer, Schlossberg, Himmelreich, Sonnuhr, Roylay.

UNTERMOSEL

Bruttig	Kochem	Rathausberg, Kuckucksberg, Johannesberg.
Kochem	Kochem	Schlossberg, Räuschel, Rosenberg.
Pünderich	Zell	Rosenberg, Marienberg, Falkenlay, Goldlay, Petersberg.
Senheim	Zell	Lay, Eulenkopf, Kuckucksbusch.
Valwig	Kochem	Herrenberg, Schwarzenberg.
Winningen	Koblenz	Hamm, Uhlen, Rosenberg.

SAAR AND RUWER

Ayl	Saarburg	Kupp, Herrenberg.
Eitelsbach	Trier (Ruwer)	Karthäuserhofberg, Marienholz.
Filzen	Saarburg	Herrenberg.
Grünhaus	Trier (Ruwer)	Maximin Gründhäuser, Herrenberg, Bruderberg, Abstberg.
Kanzem	Saarburg	Sonnenberg, Wolfsberg, Altenberg, Hörecker, Unterberg, Kelterhaus.
Kassel	Trier (Ruwer)	Blindenberg, Herrenberg, Steinkaul, Dominikanerberg, Paulinsberg, Kernagel, Hitzlay, Taubenberg, Nie'schen.

SAAR AND RUWER (*cont.*)

Villages	Districts	Best Vineyards
Oberemmel	Trier (Saar)	Falkensteiner, Junkerberg, Rosenberg, Rauler.
Ockfen	Saarburg	Neuwies, Bockstein, Herrenberg, Geisberg, Heppenstein.
Saarburg		Rausch, Leyenkaul, Antoniusbrunnen, Mühlenberg, Niederleukener Kupp.
Scharzhot	Saarburg	Scharzberg, Scharzhofberg.
Serrig	Saarburg	Vogelsang, Heiligenborn, Hindenburglay, Herrenberg, Marienberg, Würtzberger.
Waldrach	Trier (Ruwer)	Ehrenberg, Laurentiusberg, Krone.
Wawern	Saarburg	Herrenberg, Ritterpfad, Jesuitenberg, Goldberg.
Wiltingen	Saarburg	Rosenberg, Klosterberg, Dohr, Schlossberg, Kupp, Gottesfuss, Braunfels, Braune Kupp.

NAHE

Bad Kreuznach	Kreuznach	Kronenberg, Narrenkappe, Mönchberg, Brüches, Krötenpfuhl, St Martin, Rosengarten, Hinkielstein.
Burgsponheim	Kreuznach	Schlossberg, Sonnenberg.
Heddesheim	Kreuznach	Kilb, Steingerüst, Honigberg, Goldloch, Höll, Scharlachberg.
Langenlonsheim	Kreuznach	Steinchen, Dautenborn, Rotenberg.
Münster	Kreuznach	Pittersberg, Kapellenberg.
Niederhausen	Kreuznach	Rosenheck, Hermannshöhle, Steinwingert.
Norheim	Kreuznach	Delchen, Schmalberg, Hinterfels, Kufels.
Schloss Böckelheim	Kreuznach	Kupfergrube, Felsenberg, Mühlberg.
Winzerheim	Kreuznach	Honigberg, Rosenheck, Kranzgraben.

RHEINGAU

Villages	Districts	Best Vineyards
Assmannshausen		Hinterkirch, Höllenberg, Spitzerstein.
Eltville		Steinmächer, Sandgrub, Ehr, Sonnenberg, Monchhanach.
Erbach-am-Rhein		Honigberg, Hohenrain, Rheinhell, Steinmorgen, Marcobrunn, Brühl.
Geisenheim		Stainnacker, Katzenloch, Lickerstein, Rothenberg, Decker, Morschberg.
Hallgarten		Schönhell, Deitelsberg, Würzgarten.
Hattenheim		Steinberg, Nussbrunnen, Kloster Eberbach, Wisselbrunnen, Engelmannsberg.
Hochheim-am-Main		Dom-Dechaney, Kirchenstück, Stein, Daubhaus, Hülle, Falkenberg.
Johannisberg		Erntebringer, Kochsberg, Schlossberg, Schloss Johannisberg, Höllenkopf, Klaus, Höll.
Kiedrich		Gräfenburg, Sandgrub.
Östrich		Doosberg, Eiserberg, Klostergarten, Deez, Mühlberg, Neuberg, Lenchen.
Rauenthal		Hühnerberg, Siebenmorgen, Burggraben, Berg Edellese, Steinnacher, Bairen.
Rüdesheim		Bischofsberg, Burgweg, Engerweg, Häuserweg, Schlossberg, Rosenheck.
Winkel		Hasensprung, Jesuitengarten, Dachsberg, Jeonigberg, Bienengarten, Schloss Vollrads.

RHEINHESSEN

Bechtheim	Worms	Geiersberg, Katzenloch, Rosengarten.

RHEINHESSEN (*cont.*)

Villages	Districts	Best Vineyards
Bingen-am-Rhein	Bingen	Schlossberg, Schwätzerchan, Rochusberg, Rosengarten, Scharlachberg, Eisel.
Bodenheim		Burweg, Bock, Neuberg, Kahlenberg, Silberberg.
Dienheim	Oppenheim	Goldberg, Tafelstein.
Dromersheim	Bingen	Laberstall, Honigberg.
Gau-Algesheim	Bingen	Steinert, Stolzenberg, Rotenberg.
Gau-Bickelheim	Oppenheim	Goldberg, Frohngewann, Steinweg.
Gau-Odernheim	Alzey	Fuchsloch, Petersberg, Schallenberg.
Guntersblum	Oppenheim	Steinberg, Vogelgesang, Kreuz.
Laubenheim	Mainz	Berg, Edelmann, Kalkofen, Neuberg, Häuschen.
Nackenheim	Oppenheim	Rotenberg, Fenchelberg, Engelsberg, Fritzhöll.
Nieder-Ingelheim	Bingen	Horn, Nonnenberg, Steinacker.
Nierstein	Oppenheim	Rehbach, Spiegelberg, Fuchsloch, Hipping, Auflangen, Orbel, Heiligenbaum, Glöck, Domtal.
Ober-Ingelheim	Bingen	Paares, Horn, Burgweg.
Oppenheim-am-Rhein		Goldberg, Reisekahr, Sackträger, Kreuz, Krötenbrunnen, Daubhaus, Viehweg, Herrenberg.
Sprendlingen	Alzey	Geyersberg, Wiesberg, Horn, Klostergarten.
Wallertheim	Oppenheim	Wiesberg, Homberg.
Worms		Liebfrauenstift, Katterloch, Luginsland, Kirchenstück, Klostergarten.

RHEINPFALZ (PALATINATE)

Oberhaardt

Birkweiler	Landau	Schwann, Gaisberg, Herrenberg.
Burrweiler	Landau	Schöber, Altenforst, Schlossberg.

RHEINPFALZ (PALATINATE) (*cont.*)

Villages	Districts	Best Vineyards
Diesesfeld	Landau	Wetterkreuzberg, Goldmorgen, Spielfeld, Hartkopf.
Edenkoben	Landau	Mühlberg, Heiligkreuz, Klosteracker, Letten.
Hambach	Neustadt	Grain, Kirchberg, Schlossberg.
Landau-in-der-Pfalz		Löhl, Steingebiss.
Maikammer-Alsterweiler	Landau	Mandelacker, Petersbrunnen, Weinsger, Spielfeld.
St Martin	Landau	Goldmorgen, Schlossberg, Kirchberg, Spielfeld.
Siebeldingen	Landau	Hohenberg, Zelter, Sommerseite.

Mittelhaardt

Bad Dürkheim	Dürkheim	Spieberg, Hochbenn, Steinberg, Schenkenböhl, Fuchsmantel, Frohnhof, Steinböhl, Klosterberg. (Red wine) Dürkheimer Feuerberg.
Deidesheim	Neustadt	Grainhübel, Hahnenböhl, Herrgottsacker, Hofstück, Kalkofen, Kieselberg, Langenböhl, Leinhöhle, Maushöhle.
Forst	Neustadt	Kirchenstück, Ungeheuer, Jesuitengarten, Langenböhl, Freundstück, Pechstein, Schnepfenflug, Ziegler.
Gimmeldingen	Dürkheim	Hofstück, Meerspinne, Nonnengarten.
Haardt	Dürkheim	Letten, Schlossberg, Lehmgrube.
Kallstadt	Dürkheim	Steinacker, Nill, Saumagen, Kronenberg.
Königsbach	Neustadt	Mühlweg, Idig, Hinterwiese, Haag Grain, Erkernbrecht, Vogelsang.
Ruppertsberg	Dürkheim	Hofstück, Reiterpfad, Spiess, Kieselberg, Linsenbusch, Mandelacker, Gaisböhl, Mühlweg, Hoheburg.

Mittelhaardt (*cont.*)

Villages	Districts	Best Vineyards
Ungstein	Dürkheim	Herrenberg, Spielberg, Roterd.
Wachenheim	Neustadt	Mandelgarten, Luginsland, Dreispitz, Fuchsmantel, Königswingert, Wolfsdarm, Goldbächel, Gerümpel, Böhlig, Büchelein.

Unterhaardt

Dirmstein	Frankenthal	Himmelsrech, Mandelpfad, Sandacker.
Zell	Kirchheim-bolanden	Schwarzer Herrgott, Schnepfenflug, Osterberg, Philippsbrunnen.

FRANKEN (FRANCONIA)

Escherndorf	Gerolshofen	Kirchberg, Lump, Fürstenberg.
Hörstein	Alzenau	Abtsberg, Käfernberg, Langenberg.
Iphofen	Scheinfeld	Julius-Etcher-Berg, Kronsberg, Pfaffensteig.
Randersacker	Würzburg	Pfülben, Teufelskeller, Lämmerberg.
Würzburg		Schlossberg, Stein, Schalksberg, Herrenberg.

(b) Other White Wines

ALSACE In this the easternmost province of France, there is much white wine made upon the lower eastern slopes of the Vosges Mountains and well into the plain between the Vosges and the Rhine. The white wines of Alsace may be divided into two main classes, those which are made from Elbing and Burger grapes, common species that yield common wines for the common thirst of the people; and those that are made from the Sylvaner, Pinot Gris, Riesling, and Traminer or Gewurztraminer species of grapes, noble plants that give nobler fruit from which some excellent white wines are made.

The vineyards of Alsace are divided into Upper and Lower Alsace, the first being those of the Colmar district, nearer to Basle, and the second nearer to Strasbourg and Lorraine. The wines of Alsace are usually sold under the names of the grapes from which they were made, coupled with the name of the village where the winemaker has his home, cellar and winery, such as Riesling of Riquewihr, or Traminer of Ribeauvillé. The best vineyards of Upper Alsace are the following: Ammerschwihr, Beblenheim, Bergheim, Eguisheim, Guebwiller, Hunawihr, Ingersheim, Jungholtz, Katzenthal, Kayersberg, Kientzheim, Mittelwihr, Ribeauvillé (or Rappoltsweiler), Riquewihr, Rouffach, Thann, Turckheim, Wintzenheim.

And those of Lower Alsace: Audlau, Barr, Chatenois, Dambach, Epfig, Gertwiller, Goxwiller, Helifenstein, Kintzheim, Mittelbergheim, Molsheim, Obernai, Roosheim, Wolxheim.

ANJOU   The name of one of the oldest and fairest of the provinces of France, long famed for the excellence of its fruit and garden produce. The best white wines of Anjou are those which come from the vineyards of the department of Maine-et-Loire, no mean wine-producing department, since its average annual production is 15 million gallons of wine.

Most of the Anjou wines are white wines, some of which are made into sparkling wines and the others drunk very young as table wines. But there are also some very fine white wines made in the department of Maine-et-Loire, wines of rare breed and charm, which possess and retain for a number of years a kind of honey-like sweetness as distinctive as it is attractive.

The best white wines of Anjou are those of the *Coteaux de la Loire*, first among them La Coulée de Serrant, La Roche aux Moines, and Château de Savennières; and of the *Coteaux du Layon*, the best known of all being Quart de Chaume, and other first-class vineyards, those of Faye, Beaulieu, and Bonnezeaux. There are also some very pleasing Anjou *vins rosés*.

BARSAC   The white wines of Barsac are made from the vineyards of the *commune* of that name, the largest of the white wine *communes* of the Gironde, after Sauternes. Many of the white wines of Barsac are a fuller and richer edition of the type of white wines produced in the near-by district of Graves, but there are other white wines of Barsac which are of very fine quality, luscious, and fragrant, like the best wines of Sauternes, yet with a distinctively drier finish. The two best white wines of Barsac are those of Château Climens and Château Coutet; the next best are those of the Château de Myrat, Doisy-Dubroca, Doisy-Daene, Védrines, Broustet-Nairac, Cantegril, Suau, and Caillou.

BORDEAUX The vinelands of Bordeaux produce a very considerable quantity of still white wines, as well as a very small quantity of sparkling wines; these are neither better nor worse than the majority of wines which are made into sparkling wines in many parts of the world. The same cannot be said of the still white wines, as they include the white wines of Sauternes and Barsac, wines which are naturally luscious and delicious and in a class by themselves among the wines of the world. They also include the white wines of Graves, wines which enjoy a far greater measure of favour than some people think they deserve. Lastly they include white wines made in all parts of the Gironde, chiefly in the Entre-Deux-Mers district between the Garonne and the Dordogne.

BURGUNDY The best-known white wines of Burgundy are those of Chablis, but the best, as regards quality of body and bouquet, are the white wines of the Côte d'Or department. The finest of these is the wine of *Le Montrachet*, certainly the finest dry white wine of France, dry as opposed to the lusciousness of the wine of Yquem and other Sauternes, but by no means acid nor even austere. It is a wine that possesses so great a measure of dignity that it may be called majesty. Of course, there is but very little of it, and very few people in the world ever get the chance to see and drink such a wine. Next to this superlative wine from vineyards in the immediate vicinity, come the wines *Le Chevalier-Montrachet*, *Bâtard-Montrachet*, and *Demoiselles-Montrachet*, which do not possess quite the same degree of excellence, but are for all that far finer white wines than those which other wine-growers, in France and elsewhere, can ever hope to produce. There are also some very good white Burgundies made from the vineyards of Meursault, Puligny, and Chassagne. There is also a small quantity of white *Corton*, white *Morey-Saint-Denis* and white *Clos de Vougeot* made. South of the Côte d'Or, but still well within the boundaries of the ancient province of Burgundy, a fair quantity of white wines are produced every year, such as the wines of Chagny, Rully and Mâcon, but none better known than those sold under the name of *Pouilly-Fuissé*, a different wine from that of *Pouilly-Fumé*, which is a white wine from the upper reaches of the Loire.

CHABLIS   Although Chablis is one of the wine-producing districts of Burgundy, it deserves a place of its own; its popularity is greater than that of any of the other white wines of Burgundy. The real Chablis – and no other wine has suffered to the same extent from that most objectionable form of flattery called imitation – is of the palest amber in colour, with the faintest greenish tinge in it. All full colour, deep gold and even brown wines offered under the name of Chablis can be declined with thanks and finality; they are fakes. Genuine Chablis is never cheap; there is too little of it. Faked Chablis is always too dear, whatever its cost. All true Chablis is sold under the name of some shipper of repute, and all the best wines of the district of Chablis also bear the name of the vineyard from which they were made, the best of which are: *Clos, Valmur, Vaudésir, Grenouilles, Blanchot, Pointes de Preuses, Vaulorent, Bougros, Fourchaume, Montée de Tonnerre et Mont-de-Milieu.*

The official *Appellations d'origine contrôlées et réglementées* granted to the wines of Chablis are: (1) Chablis Grand Cru or Grand Chablis, for the best; (2) Chablis Premier Cru, for the second best; (3) Chablis, for fair wines from near-by vineyards; (4) Petit Chablis or Bourgogne des environs de Chablis, for lesser quality wines of near-by vineyards. *Village* and *Petit*

Village are just fancy names without any guarantee of quality.

CHÂTEAU GRILLET   A very famous white wine of which there is but a very small quantity made each year from steep terraced vineyards above Condrieu, on the right bank of the Rhône, below Lyon.

COLARES   The name of the white wines from the many vineyards upon the slopes of the hills round Lisbon which form the lower valley of the river Tagus. They are agreeable wines on the spot, upon a hot summer's day, but they are not wines of real distinction, and their chief attraction is – or used to be – their most reasonable price.

DEBRO   One of the best white wine-producing centres of Hungary.

DEZALEY   The white wine of Switzerland (Canton de Vaud) with the greatest reputation. It has little bouquet but much vinosity and a somewhat austere, flinty finish, quite distinctive as well as pleasing.

GRAVES   The white wines of the Graves district proper are those from vineyards close to Bordeaux, on the left bank of the River Garonne, north of the Sauternes district and south of the Médoc. The name Graves, however, is derived from the gravel soil of that district, and as there are other wine-producing areas which claim to have similar gravel soil, they also claim that they are entitled to call their gravel-grown wines by the name of Graves. The difficulty is not so much for the growers of the Graves de Bordeaux to prove their sole right to a name which has been theirs alone for centuries past, as to define what makes their white wines more remarkable than many other white wines of a similar type which are produced in different parts of the world. The white wines of a few particularly favoured estates, such as Châteaux Carbonnieux, Haut-Brion and Olivier, are really good, but the majority are just pleasant wines, not sweet like the Sauternes, nor have they got the breed of the Sauternes, but they are not dry like true Chablis. They are inexpensive, or ought to be.

HERMITAGE The white wine of the Hermitage, one of the most famous of the Valley of the Rhône wines, had once upon a time a world-wide reputation. After the phylloxera, the vineyards of Hermitage went out of cultivation, but they have been replanted since and white Hermitage is once more obtainable.

SAUTERNES The white wines of Sauternes are the most luscious of all natural white wines. They are made from grapes grown within a small area, south of Bordeaux, adjoining the Graves vineyards, within the limits of the *communes* or parishes of Sauternes, Bommes, Barsac, Preignac, and Fargues. The wines of Sauternes, made in good years, when the grapes are full to overflowing of sweet sunshine, are golden in colour, sweet of taste, crisp and full of grape flavour. They are quite in a class by themselves and admirable. The finest of all Sauternes wines is that of Château Yquem, always with the qualifying clause, 'of a good vintage'. In a year when the rain sets in at the time of the picking of the grapes, it is impossible to gather the Sauternes grapes in the state they must be in to give fine wine – that is, over-ripe and yet sound. In a wet vintage the alternative is to pick unripe or insufficiently ripe grapes, before they have been ruined, or become sodden and rotten grapes of no use to anybody, even if gathered from Yquem vines. After Yquem, the best or First Growths of Sauternes are: Châteaux La Tour-Blanche, Peyraguey, Vigneau, Suduiraut, Coutet, Climens, Bayle-Guiraud, Rieussec and Rabaud. The next best, and very fine they are in good years, are the wines of the following Châteaux: Myrat, Doisy, d'Arche, Filhot, Brousset-Nairac, Caillou, Suau, de Malle, Romer, and Lamothe. The wines of the parish of St Pierre-de-Mons, a little outside the Sauternes area proper, are similar to those of Sauternes, and they possess the saving grace of being less expensive.

III. PINK OR ROSÉ WINES

All the really great wines of the world are either red or white, and in the proportion of about seventy-five per cent reds to twenty-five per cent whites. But the really great wines are, like the really great people, a very small fraction of the immense flow of common, or less distinguished, wines which year after year never fail to surge forth from all the vinelands of Europe, Africa, America, and Australia, not to mention Asia, where viticulture is greatly encouraged by the Soviet administration in most parts of Russia in Asia. A comparatively small quantity of this world production of ordinary beverage wines is pink in colour, pretty to look at, pleasant to drink, but as soon forgotten as the thirst which they help to quench.

Pink wines are made differently in different parts. The best of them are made in the Rhône valley, at and near Tavel, across the river from Avignon. It looks like raspberry vinegar but it has a pleasing bouquet, no trace of acetic acid on either nose or palate, a fruity, distinctly vinous flavour, and yet so little apparent power or alcoholic strength that many who meet a Tavel rosé for the first time enjoy it by the tumblerful as they would any soft drink, soon to find that they are no longer steady on their legs or very clear in their speech. Tavel and all rosé wines are best served chilled, at the same temperature as white wines. They are best for lunch and with either fish or white meats, best also in the summer rather than in the winter.

There are pink wines made from black grapes, the white juice of which is not allowed to be in contact with the black skins of the grapes for more than a short while after fermentation sets in. In the majority of cases, however, pink wines are made from both red and white wines blended together in the right proportion to obtain just the shade of pink desired; or else from black and white grapes gathered and pressed at the same time. A large quantity of such wine used to be made in Württemberg and Baden; it was the common drink of the people, and was called Schillerwein.

There is yet another sort of pink wine, which is merely any

kind of white wine with just enough cochineal added to it to make it blush. Cochineal dye is harmless enough, and tasteless as well, but its use in wine is not to be recommended.

In France, the *vins rosés* which have been accorded the *Appellation d'origine contrôlée* are as follows:

Anjou	Coteaux du Layon
Arbois	Coteaux de la Loie
Bandol	Côtes du Jura
Beaujolais	Côtes du Rhône
Bellet	Lirac
Bourgogne	Mâcon
Bourgueil	Palette
Cassis	Saumur
Chinon	Tavel
Coteaux de l'Aubance	Touraine

There are many other white and pink table wines made from grapes grown in the vineyards of North and South America, more particularly in the U.S.A. in California and some of the eastern states in the North; in Chile and the Argentine in the South; also in Australia, chiefly in South Australia, Victoria and New South Wales; also in Africa in the Cape Province of South Africa, and in Algeria, Tunisia and Morocco in North Africa.

Fortified Wines or Wines Served at the End of a Meal

When freshly gathered ripe grapes are pressed, if their juice is left alone it ferments, which means that its sugar, or sugars – for, to be precise, there are two distinct forms of sugar in grape juice – undergo a complete change, being split up into a number of different matters, of which by far the two more important are carbonic acid gas, which escapes into the air, and ethyl alcohol, which remains and makes all the difference between grape juice and wine. When the sun has not been too kind and the grapes are not as sweet as they might be – and ought to be – the whole of their sugar content will not yield more than 8 or 9 per cent of alcohol, and the wine from such grapes will be a poor weakling on the verge of the vinegar tub. It may be acceptable, however, while still quite young, as a thirst remover, in fairly large draughts, served cool or cold, but it will not last, and it can never hope to become a fine wine. If the grapes are sweeter, because they happen to be riper or of a better species, and again if their sweet juice is allowed to ferment in its own sweet way, the wine will contain more alcohol, 10 to 12 per cent, which is the normal strength of most beverage wines, and up to 13 or 14 per cent, which is rather exceptional in all but great vintage years; there are even times when a wine may, under particularly favourable conditions, contain as much as 15 per cent of alcohol as a result of the natural fermentation of its original sweet grape juice. But, however rich in sugar any grape juice may be, fermentation stops automatically the moment the wine reaches a strength of fifteen degrees of alcohol or even before it gets there. This is nature's own thermostat system.

Ever since the time when Mr Gladstone was Chancellor of

the Exchequer, in 1860–62, wines have been taxed according to their alcoholic strength instead of according to their country of origin only; the demarcation line between the higher and lower rates of duties is intended to divide natural or beverage wines from fortified or dessert wines. Wines imported from any of the Commonwealth vineyards pay the lower rate of duty if they do not exceed 27 degrees, and the higher rate if over 27 degrees and not exceeding 42 degrees, which is the limit recognized by the Customs in Great Britain beyond which a wine ceases to be entitled to the name of wine and becomes a cordial. Wines which are imported from any part of the world other than the Commonwealth pay the lower rate of duty provided their alcoholic strength does not exceed 25 degrees, and the higher rate from 25 to 42 degrees. It is not easy to find a scientific explanation for the difference of two degrees of alcohol in favour of grapes grown under greater sunshine, and all there is to it is to accept it as being the law of the land. But what can and should be explained is the relation between degrees of alcohol and of proof spirit.* The Customs deal in degrees of proof spirit which corresponds to a little more than half alcohol and little less than half water, so that when we say that a wine may contain up to 15 per cent of alcohol after fermentation, without any outside help, the Customs refer to it as containing 27 per cent of proof spirit, or 27 degrees. This proportion of alcohol – or proof spirit, whichever name one chooses for it – is the highest that grape juice rich in sugar can reach under favourable conditions, through natural fermentation. Any wine which contains more than this proportion of alcohol has been fortified or assisted by distilled spirit added to it at some stage or other,

* *Proof Spirit:* in the United Kingdom proof spirit is 'that which at the temperature of 51° F. weighs exactly "12/13 of an equal measure of distilled water"'. This means that at a temperature of 60° F. proof spirit contains 49.28 per cent by weight or 57.10 per cent by volume of alcohol. Any degree or degrees of alcohol over or under 57.10 by volume is stated with the mention 'o.p.' or 'u.p.', meaning 'over proof' or 'under proof'. Thus a spirit containing 60.6 of alcohol, by volume, and another 53.8, would be described as: the first 3.5 o.p.; and the second, 3.3 u.p.

T–D

early or late, of its fermentation. The spirit thus added to raise the alcoholic strength of wine should be – and it usually is – distilled from wine, so that the addition is of wine in one form to wine in another form.

Strange as it may seem, the addition of brandy to wine is not done in the more northern vineyards, where the grapes do not always ripen fully, and where the wines are liable to lack body and power. To help such wines as these, more particularly in sunless seasons, sugar is sometimes added to the grapes at the time of the pressing in order that the alcoholic strength of the wine may eventually reach ten per cent, or a little more if possible. But as the chief charm of all the wines from the more northern vineyards is their delicacy and discreet bouquet, to add brandy would ruin them altogether. What long experience has shown to be well worth while is the addition of brandy to the stouter wines of Portugal, Spain, Madeira, Sicily, and other wines of a similar type made under similar climatic conditions, in the Americas, South Africa and Australia. These wines are made from over-ripe grapes or, at any rate, grapes which have a very high sugar content, more sugar than they can use up in the natural process of fermentation, and the addition of brandy stabilizes their excess of grape sugar; it remains present to tone down the fire of the added brandy, which, in its turn, removes any cloying mawkishness due to an excess of grape sugar – quite a happy partnership.

The best and, in England, the best-known fortified wines are (1) Port, (2) Sherry, (3) Madeira, (4) Marsala.

I. PORT

Port is a fortified wine, made from grapes grown in the Upper Valley of the Douro, and shipped from Oporto. This is the legal definition of Port, but it would be rash and wrong to imagine that Port is just a type of wine always more or less the same. There are many different wines, golden, tawny, and of the deepest purple, which all conform to the above specifications, and yet are not at all alike in colour, flavour, bouquet and strength.

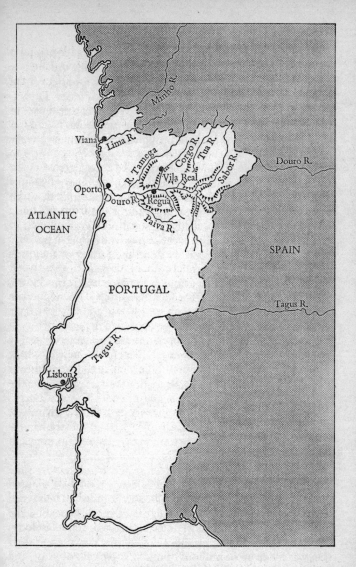

The Port District

The Douro is a river which rises in Spain, enters Portugal at a place called Barca d'Alva, and loses itself in the Atlantic at S. João da Foz, just below the twin towns of Oporto, on the right bank, and Vila Nova de Gáia, on the opposite one. During its passage through Portugal, the Douro runs – at a mad pace in the winter and spring of the year, but in a leisurely fashion during the summer months – through some 240 miles of vine-lands.

There are in the Douro Valley some 65,000 acres of vines, and they yield on an average about 100,000 pipes of Douro wine, by no means all of it Port Wine. Port Wine must do more than come from Douro-grown grapes; it must be made in a certain manner. As in all wines, the quality of Port depends in the first place on the quality of the grapes from which it is made, but it also depends appreciably upon the quality of the spirit used to fortify it, and upon the amount of such spirit and upon the time when it is added to the fermenting wine. But Port is not a blend of grape juice and wine spirit; it is a wine, the fermented juice of ripe grapes, fermented in a peculiar manner which experience has proved to be the most suitable.

The vines from which Port is made are grown in vineyards above Regoa, which is a long way inland from Oporto, where the granite subsoil of the coastal hills is replaced by a schistous formation. As soon as the grapes are ripe they are pressed, on the spot, in the *lagar* of the nearest *quinta*, or estate. *Lagars* are large, square, stone troughs, and as soon as a *lagar* is filled with grapes, a crowd of unshaven ruffians, barelegged and mostly bandy-legged, step in and perform a kind of bear dance, jumping and swaying about, to the tune of music of sorts, singing out of tune something which sounds like a dirge but is meant to be the praises of Bacchus. Soon the whole *lagar* is a mass of discoloured husks in a sea of purple juice, the juice of the grapes. Their work done, and it is hard work indeed, the men go home, and the must, or grape juice, is left in peace. Its peace does not last long. When the grapes were picked, the fine grey down upon their skin was made up of millions of microscopic cells of yeast, and as soon as they are in contact with the sugar stored within each ripe grape berry something happens which is called fermentation. Fermentation is the natural reshuffling of the carbon, hydrogen and oxygen which make up grape sugars, resulting in the formation of ethyl alcohol, which remains in the grape juice that was and now becomes wine, and carbonic acid gas, which loses itself in the air. This does not happen all at once; it takes quite a while for the whole of the sugars in grape-juice to be all used up by fermentation, and in the making of Port man intervenes to check fermentation at a time when there are still plenty of grape sugars left. This checking is done by adding some distilled wine, or brandy; the alcoholic strength of the new wine is then too high for fermentation to proceed.

The marriage of two such cousins as immature wine, or partly fermented and fermenting grape juice, on the one hand, and fiery wine, in the shape of fully fermented wine which has been distilled into spirit, on the other, would not be approved of, nor would it prove to be a success, in other vinelands; yet experience has shown that it happened to suit the temperament and character of the Douro grapes. But, and this is a very important But, the newly wed couple must be given time to get used to one another, to live together until they will resemble one another so much that in the end it becomes impossible to tell which is which. This is a slow process which takes place in the Port shippers' lodges, at Vila Nova de Gaia, opposite Oporto, where the wines of each new vintage are sent down from the up-river vinelands when merely a few weeks old. It is there, under the ever-vigilant eye of the shipper, that young wines are trained, matched and watched, with the help of a little more brandy if and when needed, but chiefly through mixing with good company, older wines, or wines from different vineyards, and possessing just that particularly good quality that the youngster may be lacking.

After the grapes, and the brandy added to the new wine, the most important factor in the making of Port is the shipper. Many there are who even argue that the Port shipper is more important than all else: so much depends upon his judgement, his skill, and, of course, his stocks of wine and brandy. One may prefer an early bottled vintage Port to a light tawny Port, from the wood, or *vice versa*. But whatever style of Port happens to be preferred does not affect the truth of the saying that the best Port is the best blend of Port, hence the best Port shippers are the best blenders of Port. To be a Port shipper one must have more than one's name on a brass plate and an address at Oporto or Vila Nova de Gaia; one must also have stocks of Port wines of various, and good, vintages. All the leading Port shippers own considerable stocks of Port wines, and most of them also own vineyards in the Upper Douro, estates or *quintas*, the names of some of which are well known to Port lovers in England. Such, for instance, are the Quinta de Roriz, Boa Vista, Noval, Tua, Malvedos, Zimbro, Bomfim and a few more.

If we consider that besides the differences in the quality of the grapes vintaged each year, differences which are due to climatic conditions, Port shippers have in their lodges more Ports in reserve than there are letters in the alphabet, we shall easily realize that there must be – and indeed there are – many different types and qualities of Port. Most of them, however, fall into two main categories, according to whether they are the wines of one vintage or a blend of several years; and then they can also be subdivided according to whether the wine has been aged in cask or in bottle. The names under which most Ports are offered for sale are: *vintage*, *tawny* and *ruby*, all of them made from black grapes. There is also a White Port, which is never white but deep amber or light tawny in colour. White Port is never bottled early but matured in wood; it is mostly rather sweet, and sometimes very sweet.

Vintage Port. Vintage Port is the wine of any one year; it is normally shipped two years after the vintage, occasionally in the third year. A vintage Port is bottled very soon after it arrives, being left to mature in bottle for a number, sometimes a great number, of years. The characteristics of any vintage Port are the characteristics of the year when the grapes were gathered and the wine made: it is not for the shipper to decide whether he is going to make his wine into a very big vintage year that will take a very long time to reach perfection or a lighter vintage year which will be ready for drinking at a much earlier date. This depends entirely upon the amount and incidence of rain and sunshine, moisture and temperature, during the year, and more particularly from the flowering of the vines until the gathering of the grapes. But what the shipper can and does decide for himself is whether he will ship the wine of the year as a vintage or not. There are exceptional years when the quality and abundance of the grapes are such that there is no hesitation possible and all shippers ship a more or less considerable proportion of the wine they make as a vintage. But the Oporto shippers have not had many such years during the last quarter of a century. There have been a number of good years in the Douro, but they have not been extraordinarily good, not so good as regards both quality and quantity that every shipper without exception could not possibly help shipping his wine as a vintage. It has been a question for each individual shipper to decide for himself what was the best thing to do, whether or not to ship the wine of the year as a vintage and, if so, what quantity of the year's wine he should ship as a vintage, retaining whatever quantity of the wine he needs for maturing in his Oporto Lodges and for refreshing the older wines he keeps there.

Late Bottled Vintage Port. A vintage Port is the wine of different vineyards but made in any one year, a good year, a vintage year, and it is usually bottled early, not later than three years from the date of the vintage when the grapes were gathered. But there are exceptions to all rules. A vintage Port may be the wine of one estate or *quinta* bottled early. A vintage Port may also be and sometimes is kept in cask for ten, twelve and fifteen years before being bottled. Such a wine, which is known as late bottled vintage Port, will be lighter in colour and body than the early bottled vintage wine, but, after it has been bottled a little time, it will develop a vintage nose or bouquet which no tawny Port will ever have.

Tawny Port. The difference between vintage and tawny Port is that the first is the wine of a single year and is matured in bottle, while the second is a blend of the wine of several years and is matured in cask.

Some of the wine made in moderate years, wine that is not suitable for bottling as vintage Port, may blend very happily with other wines and hold its own most honourably in the assembly of the various vintages which go to make a good tawny Port. But the best tawny Port is necessarily the best blend, and the best blend will always be made of the best wines.

Thus the shipper who has a large demand for fine tawny Port may decide not to ship as a vintage the wine of a year which is quite up to vintage standard if it is also the wine which he wants to keep up the standard of his tawny Port of various marks. This is the reason why there is not more unanimity among Port shippers in the matter of the shipping of vintage Ports.

Tawny Port is a blend of Ports matured in wood. It acquires its peculiar tawny colour through the precipitation of the red colouring pigment present in the mucilage of the grape skins: as the wine ages in casks – that is to say, in the presence of a fairly free supply of oxygen – a series of chemical changes takes place slowly but continuously, the wine becoming oxidized to a certain degree, and when you look at it in a glass you find, after the wine has been in cask some years, that its purple colour has brightened up to the burning red of clear ruby; leave it in cask longer and you will find the ruby mantle of your wine glowing with a subdued tinge of gold and hemmed with a faint hem of rust-like amber.

Ruby Port. A late bottled vintage Port may be ruby in colour, but the wine known as ruby Port is usually a blend of wines of different vintages, young vintages as a rule, although there is such a wine as an old *Ruby*, a blend of wines, the youngest of which may be as much as ten years old, and still retaining its deep vintage colour.

A blend, when we speak of ruby or tawny Port, means something very different from the way coffee and milk are poured in the same cup to make *café au lait*. When wines of different years find themselves in the same cask, they do not blend there and then. They take quite a long time to marry, hence the absolute necessity of giving them time and rest in cask before bottling them.

Once in bottle, tawny Port had much better be sold for immediate consumption; it will give more satisfaction than if allowed to age in bottle for it is not likely to improve: it may even go out of condition. Ruby Port, on the other hand, will repay being kept for four or five years, because it will throw a crust and there are a great many people who love a crusted Port, although they cannot afford or will not pay the price of old vintage Port.

Tawny Port and ruby Port are beautiful wines. They have not got the body nor the bouquet of the vintage wines, but they possess a most seductive delicacy and the silkiest touch; they are soothing and refreshing. But they are not cheap. They are dear and cannot help being dear. They are matured for many years in cask and in lodges at Oporto, where the evaporation averages about $2\frac{1}{2}$ per cent per annum; this means that in twenty-five years you only have fifty pipes instead of a hundred, fifty pipes which cost you the price you paid for a hundred, plus the interest on your money during twenty-five years, to say nothing of rent, insurance and the care given to the wine during all that time.

There is a short cut to something that resembles the true tawny colour; it is a blend of young white and red Ports. But short cuts, in the matter of Ports, are avoided by all wise people.

II. SHERRY

Sherry is a wine of many moods and tenses, the most popular of which happen to be in Great Britain at the present time the driest forms, the Finos, Amontillado, Montilla, and Manzanilla, which are best as aperitifs, served before meals, and are also acceptable and enjoyable, well chilled, as table white wines,

especially when highly spiced sauces or dishes are being served.★
But Sherry can also be served after or at the end of dinner with
dessert, fruit, or sweets. After-dinner Sherry has the unique
advantage among wines of being enjoyed even when the
smoke of cigars and cigarettes has made its unwelcome but
nowadays inevitable appearance.

The finest after-dinner Sherries are the *Oloroso* and *Amoroso*
types of Sherry which have had the benefit of some years in
bottle. In degree of sweetness and in colour, after-dinner
Sherries vary greatly, which is only natural since they owe both
their sweetness and colour to the skill and fancy of every individual shipper. It would be wrong, however, to imagine that
Sherries are coloured or sweetened artificially, since both
colouring and sweetening agents used are also wines, Spanish
wines, which are either very sweet indeed or very dark.

The finest and dearest of sweet Spanish wines used to sweeten
after-dinner Sherries is known as P.X., being the initials of
Pedro Ximenez, the Spanish form of the name of a German called
Peter Siemens, who is credited with introducing to the *vignerons* of Andalusia the species of white grape which has borne his
name ever since. They are very sweet grapes, lacking in acidity,
and when they are picked, at the time of the vintage, they are
left exposed to the heat of the sun until they become almost like
raisins; they are then pressed and their very sweet juice runs
straight from the press into butts already quarter-filled with
brandy, so that their juice has no chance at all even to start fermenting. It is more of a liqueur than a wine, and when a little
is added to a dry Sherry it rounds off all corners in a truly
admirable manner, giving it a softer finish as well as greater
strength, but no darker colour.

Old Brown Sherries, which were in great demand in Victorian times, and most after-dinner Sherries to this day are given
a darker, deeper shade of brown-gold, by the addition of more or
less *vino de color*. Again, this 'wine of colour' is no wine at all,
but grape juice which never was given any chance to ferment.
Its fermentation, however, is not checked at the outset, as in the

★ See Aperitif Wines, p. 22.

case of the P.X., by brandy, but by heat: it is slowly simmered down before fermentation sets in either to a third or a fifth of its original volume; if to one third it is called *sancocho*, if to a fifth *arrope*, and in each case it acquires a dark brown colour in the process of cooking, and it looks more like treacle than wine. Diluted with some old wine, it is known as *vino de color* and used to impart to after-dinner Sherries greater sweetness, deeper colour, but no greater strength.

There is a place near Arcos which is called Pajarete where they probably initiated the practice of blending P.X. and *vino de color*, both very sweet, but the first having strength and the second colour. This combination, which used to be in great demand in the days when dark and sweet after-dinner Sherries were first favourites, is now made anywhere in the south of Spain, but it is still known, wherever it is made, by the name of *Pajarete*. Both Pedro Ximenez and vino de color, as well as their offspring Pajarete, are expensive forms of wine; they are really concentrates, used with discretion and only for sweetening, colouring, and improving the better types of after-dinner Sherries. The cheaper wines are sweetened and coloured by a wine called *Dulce apagado*, which is a blend of young and raw spirit at very high strength added to the must or freshly pressed grape juice of common grapes.

It is but rarely that the wines of any one vintage are kept to themselves at Jerez, and the name *solera*, followed by the date of a year, does not mean that the year given is that of the vintage when the grapes were picked from which the wine in the bottle has been made. *Solera* does not mean vintage, but soil, in the sense of foundation, that upon which the quality of the wine stands. Each type of wine in the shipper's *bodega* is lodged in butts piled one upon two others, in three tiers and sometimes four, the oldest wine being in the lowest butts, the wines of more recent vintages being kept in the butts nearest the ceiling. When the shipper requires some of the type of wine lodged in two or three of his *soleras* – there are *soleras* of Finos, Olorosos, and even *vinos de color* – he draws a small quantity from each of the lowest butts, those on the soil or floor of the *bodega*, and what he draws is then made good from the wine of the butts immediately above, which in their turn, are also filled from the topmost butts. This system may go on for many years without the *solera* being run out and another start being made. When a year is given immediately after the word *solera* it is intended to be the date when the particular *solera* was first laid down from which the wine in the bottle was made up.

III. MADEIRA

Madeira is the wine made from the finest grapes grown in the island of Madeira: it is fortified and matured in Madeira before being sold.

There was a time, far away back in the seventeenth century, when England jealously guarded all commercial intercourse with the West Indies and the mainland of Northern America for her own nationals; a time when nothing that had been grown or manufactured in Europe was allowed to be shipped to the Plantations and Colonies except from English ports, in English-owned ships. This ukase was hard upon the wine-growers of France, Spain, Germany, Portugal and Italy, but it was far more unfair to the unfortunate colonists on the other side of the Atlantic, men who were fighting against very great odds for the sake of the motherland, and who could not get a drop of wine, except at fantastic prices, to cheer them on. They would have either died or else returned to England, had it not been for the happy thought of the man who told the king that Madeira was in Africa; not being of European growth, the wine of Madeira could be and was shipped to America. English merchants soon saw and took their chance. They migrated to Madeira and had no difficulty in getting the natives to pull up their sugar-canes and to replace them with vines. There had been vines grown there long before, but only on a small scale, for the needs of the islanders, but during the last quarter of the seventeenth and the whole of the eighteenth centuries the making of wine was the best-paying industry of the island. During all that time Madeira wine was shipped to all sorts of places in small quantities, but the bulk and the best of the wines made there all went west to Boston, New York, Philadelphia, or Savannah, and all along the Atlantic seaboard of Northern America.

The fact that the wines of Madeira were first shipped to America in large quantities is only one of the reasons why the best Madeiras are to be found in the United States even now. The other reason is that Madeira wine was understood in America as it has never been understood elsewhere. Being for quite a long time the only wine one could obtain with ease, much attention was paid to it, much more than any other wine has ever received, and it was soon discovered that Madeira is quite different from other wines and requires to be treated differently. It wants more air to breathe, to live and expand, than other wines. So they used to send their Madeiras for long sea trips, and when it came home they stored it in large demijohns, not in cellar cool, but in the loft, under the roof, where it would have plenty of air, and where it would also feel like all the members of the family – only rather more so – the alternatives of summer heat and winter frost. When the wine was ripe, after a respectable number of years, it was siphoned from the demijohn nearest to the one that had just seen its last wine leave it; it was passed through cheese-cloth into decanters, and even then, as its last hour was approaching, it was given more air, being left in the decanter for a day or two, sometimes even longer, before coming up before the critical tribunal of the old connoisseur's red-brick nose, to be passed on to the Palate Chamber for a short stay upon appeal and committed for life to the Court below. Madeira, in those days, when men had both taste and time, was never afflicted by the humiliation of the strait-jacket – that is, a black bottle – nor the impure contact of a soft spongy cork, as was the fate and still is the fate of Madeira in other lands.

The chief wines of Madeira one can buy today are known by name, not of the vineyard which produced the grapes, but of the grapes themselves, either *Sercial*, *Bual*, *Verdelho*, *Terrantez*, or *Malmsey*. But there is unfortunately no guarantee that the species of vines corresponding to those names were actually the parents of the wines which bear their names. The best guarantee is the name of an old-established shipper with a long reputation behind him.

The old vines have met with more than one disaster during the last century; they give finer wine but they have not got the same power as commoner stock to stand up to disease and pests. So the wines which bear those time-honoured names, although they may not be all nor wholly entitled to call themselves by such names, are made in such a way as to possess as much as is possible the outstanding characteristics associated with each kind of vine. Thus a *Sercial* is a wine with a somewhat austere finish as well as great vinosity. It is an ideal wine for the beginning of the meal, both before, during and after soup; one cannot wish for a better foundation upon which to build an enjoyable symposium of wines. The *Malmsey* would be too rich, to begin with; it would kill the next wine, whatever might be served with fish or roast. Its proper place is in the morning, with a slice of cake, or at tea-time with a biscuit, or after dinner with fruit or even without any fruit or anything else but the joy of tasting good wine in good company, the company of friends who can either talk intelligently or listen appreciatively. The *Bual* or *Boal*, as it is spelt in Portuguese, is not nearly so unctuous as the *Malmsey*, nor has it the dry finish of the *Sercial*. Its chief attraction is its perfect balance, the harmony between bouquet, fruit, and body. It is equally enjoyable at the beginning as at the end of dinner.

The characteristic qualities of Madeira are due to vines, soil, and climate in the first place, and in the second to the fact that the wine is prepared in a manner which is unlike that which obtains in Spain, Portugal and anywhere else where fortified wines are made.

First of all the grapes are pressed and their sweet juice, called *mosto*, is conveyed as quickly as possible from the vineyards to Funchal. From the hillsides, this *mosto* is mostly brought to the lodges in goat skins, containing about 12 gallons each, by the *borracheiros*, men who walk from 12 to 15 miles in record time with a weight of about 150 lb. across their shoulders. From some vineyards on the southern slopes of the island the *mosto* is sent to the lodges at Funchal in casks, on sledges drawn by tough little oxen down the steep cobbled roads. From the northern slopes of Madeira the *mosto* is shipped in casks in sailing barks to Funchal.

When the *mosto* gets to the shipper's lodges at Funchal it ferments and becomes *vinho claro*, or new wine.

The *vinho claro* is then treated in a way which is peculiar to Madeira; it is treated by heat, in *estufas*, or hot chambers, where it is subjected to a temperature varying from 100 to 160° F., according to the length of time allowed by different shippers and for different wines. As a matter of general practice, the higher the temperature the shorter will be the wine's stay in the *estufa*. When it leaves the *estufa*, the *vinho claro* is known as *vinho estufado*.

Then the *estufado vinho* is racked, after having been given a good rest, and it becomes *trasfugado vinho*.

The *trasfugado vinho* is then fortified, or *alcoolisado*, with an average of added alcohol of some 10 per cent of its volume, by which time it has become *vinho generoso*.

Vinhos generosos are then blended among themselves first, and with the wines of former years at a later stage, before they are allotted to a number of different vattings, or *lots*, and left alone to be perfected by the greatest of all masters – Time.

The considerable amount of trouble taken with the young wines of Madeira is responsible for the fact that they will stand more rough usage and live longer than any other wine.

On the other hand, Madeira must be given time to mature; many wines, not only Moselles, but even Clarets and Champagne, can be enjoyable when quite young, but Madeira never is. Time, of course, means money; it means locked-up capital and lost interest; it means loss of wine through evaporation and ullage; it means higher insurance charges and greater risks. Hence Madeira cannot compete with other fortified wines as regards cost, but it does compete with the cheapest of all as regards values, a very different proposition.

IV. MARSALA

Marsala is the best fortified wine of Italy. It possesses a beautiful dark amber colour, more sweetness than stoutness of body, a discreet but very pleasing bouquet, and a slightly acid sub-conscious or farewell, which is more reminiscent of Madeira than Sherry, probably due to the loose volcanic soil of the vineyards which produce it.

Marsala is made from two species of white grapes, the Cataretto and Inzolia, grown in the province of Trapani, of which Marsala is the chief exporting port.

John Woodhouse, who was described at his death as 'an entirely honest wine-merchant' – and he would probably never have wished for a better epitaph – was not always a wine-merchant. He was the son of a Liverpool shipowner; he went to Sicily in 1770 to purchase and load some soda ash – the commercial anhydrous sodium carbonate – and he liked the wines of the country so much that he must have purchased some of that which was vintaged in 1770, shipping seventy pipes of it, in 1773, from Trapani to Liverpool in the good ship *Elizabeth*. Acting upon the advice of one of his friends he had two gallons of the locally distilled brandy added to each pipe of wine, before it was shipped, to fortify it against the strain and fatigue of the sea voyage. This first shipment of Trapani wine – as it was called at the time – met with so enthusiastic a reception that John Woodhouse decided to devote his energies and capital to making the wines of Trapani and Marsala the rivals of those of Madeira, then in favour in England. In 1796 he settled at Marsala, and he had no cause to regret it. The fact that merely four years later, in 1800, he was able to supply 100 pipes of Marsala wine to 'His Majesty's ships off Malta', under the command of Nelson, is sufficient evidence of the rapid growth of his business.

A few years later, in 1805, Benjamin Ingham, a Yorkshireman, settled at Palermo and devoted himself to the improvement of vine-growing and wine-making methods in Sicily. In 1813 he decided to become a wine-merchant on his own account and began to ship Marsala wines; his firm soon became a flourishing concern and a rival of John Woodhouse's. But the wines of Marsala were at the time so popular in England that there was ample room for those two men from Lancashire and Yorkshire as well as a third comer, an Italian, one Vincenzo Florio, who started business as a wine-shipper, at Marsala, in 1825, and shortly after at Trapani as well. These three firms shared the Marsala export trade until 1929, when the Florio concern took over the other two, and still is the one and only reliable source of Marsala wines. There are a number of minor Italian firms engaged in supplying cheap and nasty wines called Marsala, but such wines had better be left to the natives.

At the time of the vintage in August or, at latest, in early September, the many small vineyard owners of the province of Trapani, and of parts of the adjoining province of Palermo, pick their grapes and press them as best they can. By the following November or, at latest, December the new wine has done fermenting, and it is then racked and brought to the factory, where the raw and rough wine will be made into Marsala, after being given some tannin, to stiffen its backbone, some brandy to fortify it, some *vino cotto* to sweeten it and last, but by no means least, some time to digest all these and become true Marsala. The *vino cotto* is grape juice which has been cooked or simmered to a third of its original bulk; it is a grape-juice syrup, not really wine at all, and as it acquires in the cooking a brown or caramel colour, one may expect, as a rule, the darker Marsalas to be also the sweeter.

Marsala, the wine which will eventually leave the factory under that name, is by no means uniform in type and quality. It is made to order according to the means and the taste of the consumers thereof. The sweetest and weakest Marsalas are those which are sold under the names of *Marsaletta* and *Garibaldi*; their alcoholic strength is not above 15 degrees of alcohol, the strength of some beverage wines. The wine sold under the mark *Italia* is not quite so sweet, and its strength varies from 16 to 18 degrees. All three marks are intended for consumption in Italy. Marsalas intended for shipment overseas are marketed under various marks such as: Inghilterra, L.P. (London Particular);

O.P. (Old Particular); C.O.M. (Choice Old Marsala); S.O.M. (Superior Old Marsala). The alcoholic strength of such marks may vary from 18 to 22 degrees of alcohol, never less than 18 degrees if shipped by a reputable shipper.

The reason why Marsala destined for home consumption is so much weaker than that which is exported may be due to a difference in the taste of the consumers, but it is more likely to be the consequence of the fact that the spirit used to fortify Marsala is very heavily taxed, hence very expensive, but the tax is remitted and the spirit is correspondingly very cheap when and if it is used to fortify wines shipped overseas.

After it is given some tannin, some spirit (if it is for export) and some sweetening, Marsala is left to mature out of doors, so that it may get the benefit of the torrid heat of the summer and the cold nights of the winter in turns during three or four consecutive years, when it is generally considered to be ready for shipment and consumption.

Although as a matter of general rule Marsala is a blended, fortified, and sweetened wine, there are some quite exceptional vintages when it is neither blended, nor fortified, nor sweetened. Two such vintages were those of 1834 and 1870, the wines of which reached from 16 to 17 degrees of alcohol without any spirit having been added.

Besides its place on the dinning-room table with the dessert, Marsala is a very welcome wine in the kitchen. It is indispensable in the making of zabaglione, scallopine alla Marsala, and various other sauces and sweets.

V. OTHER FORTIFIED WINES

ALICANTE   The fortified wine made in the province of Levante, in Spain, mostly from the vineyards of Alicante, the oldest centre of wine production of this province, their yearly average output being about ten million gallons of both beverage and dessert wines. The wines of Alicante were fairly popular in England during the nineteenth century until they lost their place in popular favour to the cheaper wines of Tarragona.

BANYULS   The best of the French dessert wines. The vine-yards of Banyuls are on the French side of the Pyrenees in Roussillon, and they produce both black grapes and white grapes. The wine which is made from the red-black grapes of Banyuls is fortified when partly fermented, and it may then be left to ferment on its husks, or else away from the husks so as to obtain a rosé wine. Locally the red and rosé wines made at Banyuls are not called Banyuls but Grenache wine, from the name of the grapes. The name of Banyuls wine is given exclusively to the fortified wine made from the white grapes of Banyuls.

FRONTIGNAN   One of the sweet dessert wines of France, from the Languedoc, which enjoyed a great measure of popularity in England during the eighteenth century, when it was known as Frontigniac, Frontiniac, and Frontignac.

LISBON   The red and white wines of the lower Tagus valley, from Lisbon to the Atlantic, were fortified and shipped to England during the eighteenth century and the first half of the nineteenth, when they competed with the similar wines from Oporto, and were often as dear and even dearer than the cheaper grades of Port. They ceased to be imported when Tarragona wines came over from Spain at appreciably cheaper prices, even before Australia and South Africa also shipped fortified wines of the same type, which were admitted in Great Britain at a lower rate of duty.

MALAGA   One of the pleasantest of the dessert wines which used to be very popular in England. They were fortified wines made mostly from the Pedro Ximenez grapes, fortified and coloured with *vino de color*, like Brown Sherries. There were also some Malaga wines made from Muscat grapes and called Moscatel de Málaga, which was very luscious and the perfect 'ladies' wine' in Victorian days.

MUSCATEL   There are many wines made in different parts of the world from muscat grapes and called Muscatel. In southern California there is a great deal of Muscatel made either from white grapes such as the Burger and Sauvignon, or else from black grapes the juice of which is not allowed to ferment in contact with the skins of the grapes. It is fortified before the fermentation is over, and it is both sweet, fragrant and strong.

SITGES   The vineyards of this port, south of Barcelona, in northern Spain, produce white Muscatel grapes from which a light golden wine is made, which is not very much fortified – its strength varies from sixteen to eighteen degrees of alcohol – and is one of the nicest of Muscatel wines.

TARRAGONA   There are two distinct classes of wines made from the considerable vineyards of Tarragona: common, rough, fortified wines, a cheap imitation of Port, and pleasant muscat fortified wines highly popular as altar wines. The first have ceased to be imported in Great Britain since the preferential duties granted to the wines of Australia and South Africa, and the second are not the type of wines for which there has ever been much demand in this country.

VALENCIA   The annual average production of the vine-yards of Valencia, in the Spanish province of Levante, is about nineteen million gallons of both beverage and fortified wines; the latter are chiefly noted for their very deep red, almost black, and great strength, and they were in great demand for blending purposes before the preferential duties accorded to Empire wines.

Wines for Special Occasions

I. CHAMPAGNE

Champagne was during a great many past centuries the name of still red or white wines, some better than others of course, but none of outstanding excellence. They were mostly made from the same species of grapes as those grown in Burgundy, but their distinction came from the fact that they were produced solely from grapes grown in the vineyards of the province of Champagne, where the soil is richer in lime, and therefore much lighter than Burgundian soil, and the climate a good deal cooler than the climate of Burgundy.

It was only during the latter years of the seventeenth century, the whole of the eighteenth, and the first three quarters of the nineteenth that a comparatively small quantity of Champagne was made white and sparkling. It was invariably sweetened with sugar candy and served as a dessert wine, with sweets and fruit at the end of a meal.

Dry, sparkling Champagne, as we know it today, was first made at the demand of some of the wine-merchants of Great Britain during the last two decades of the nineteenth century. Its popularity grew so rapidly that the making of sparkling wine soon ceased to be a secret and sparkling wines with the same gas content as Champagne could be made and were made in many parts of the world and given the name of Champagne to which they had no right.

Happily, since 1960, the name Champagne is protected by the law of Great Britain, as it is in France and Germany. In the U.S.A., however, although no sparkling wine may be imported other than genuine Champagne from the vineyards of Champagne, the sparkling wines made from American-grown grapes may be sold as Champagne.

Champagne is the wine made from the grapes of a strictly limited number of vineyards, most of them in the valley of the Marne within a triangle with Reims, Épernay, and Châlons-sur-Marne as its three points.

As soon as the grapes are ready for the press and weather conditions favourable, the grapes have to be gathered very rapidly, and the vintagers, men, women, and children, scatter among the vines as thick as rooks in a newly sown field.

When the grapes reach the press-house they are weighed and pressed with as little delay as possible.

The Champagne wine-press is a square receptacle with a solid oak floor, movable oak-rail sides, and a very heavy oak lid which may be raised or lowered by means of steel screws worked by a powerful lever.

The great majority of the grapes grown in Champagne are black grapes, that is to say, their skin is purple, but their sweet juice is greenish-white. The coloured pigment of the black Pinots or Champagne grapes is in the lining of their skin alone, and with the method of pressing the grapes used in Champagne, the juice does not remain long enough in contact with the crushed skins to become red, so that a pale white wine is obtained from black grapes.

Grape juice is not appetizing to look at nor is it at all satisfactory as a drink; it is turbid, watery and very sweet. But leave it alone and it will very soon ferment; it will become more turbid, fret, then 'boil' and cool down again all of its own accord; after this much of its natural grape sugar has gone; this has been transformed by the natural phenomenon of fermentation into carbonic acid gas, which loses itself in the air, and alcohol which remains in the wine.

It is at that stage that the Champagne shipper has to intervene and show his skill; he has, in his *celliers*, hundreds or thousands of hogheads of new wine in the place of the same number of hogheads of grape juice, which he had pressed or bought some three months earlier, at the time of the vintage.

This new wine is now bright, because the cold of the winter has checked the fermentation and caused all the sediment in the wine to fall to the bottom of the casks where it forms the lees. First of all, the wine is *racked* – that is to say, drawn off its lees into fresh casks, then it is blended.

Blending is a most difficult art indeed. The shipper must judge which of the new wines from this, that, and the other vineyards will 'marry' most happily, in what proportions they ought to be blended, which should be saved for use in later years, and what quantity – if any – of wines reserved for the purpose in former years should be added to the blend or *cuvée*. Of course, if the shipper when he is selecting the wines which will go to form his *cuvée* had only to make up the most palatable blend in the same way as any tea or coffee blender, his task would be comparatively easy; what makes it so much more arduous is that he has to blend living wines which have yet their lives to live, and he has to make his *cuvée* a success not the day he blends it, but ten and fifteen years later.

When the shipper has made up his *cuvée* or *cuvées* during the winter months following the vintage, he must bottle the wine in the spring or early summer.

The first thing for the Champagne shipper to do when he is about to bottle a *cuvée* is to ascertain how much gear there is in the wine; should there be too much the corresponding quantity of carbonic acid gas produced eventually by fermentation would be too great, and would cause many bottles to burst; on the other hand, should there not be enough grape sugar left at the time of bottling, the wine would never be sufficiently sparkling.

All the bottles of a *cuvée* are filled straight from the same large vat, into which the right number of casks of different wines are emptied and thoroughly blended together. Then each bottle is immediately corked with a big cork, which has to be squeezed hard to the size of the neck of the bottle before it can be driven into it. The cork is secured by a steel hook or clamp, which makes it impossible for the cork to pop off.

Not that the cork has the slightest disposition to pop off just then, but the wine within the bottle will not remain very long as still as it is the day it is bottled.

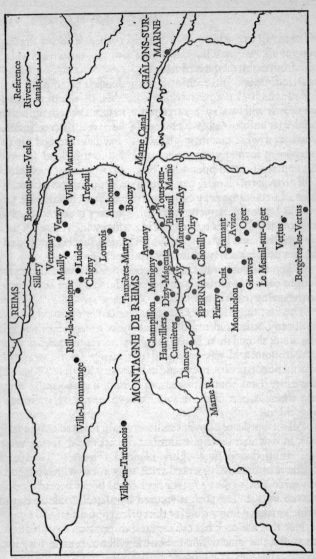

The Champagne District

The new wine is no sooner bottled than it is laid to rest in deep vaults, away from all light and noise.

The bottles are binned away, neck to neck, in a close embrace, and they are left alone for many months.

Some of the Champagne cellars are a hundred feet deep, so that the wine stored therein is quite safe from summery heatwaves as from the winter's icy spells, safe also from the rumblings of heavily loaded motor lorries and all the turmoil of the feverish outside world.

And yet, it is not at peace!

Far from it! Still, dark and damp is the grave into which each bottle of new Champagne has been lowered immediately after being corked, but the wine within its glass prison is very much alive, and it will have no rest until it is set free.

It frets and loses its brilliant complexion; it becomes sick, and after a time recovers, but it is never the same again.

What really happens is a series of complex chemical changes. The sugar present in the wine is gradually transformed by fermentation into ethyl alcohol and carbonic acid gas, and the latter, not being able to escape, remains in solution in the wine; it will only leave it when the cork of the bottle is removed and in its haste to depart from the bottle or from the glass it will cause the wine to bubble or foam.

Fermentation is not the only chemical action which goes on within each bottle of new wine, while it is left alone in the long and peaceful night of the deep Champagne cellars. There are others during which acids and sugars fight each other, and it is because of these slow but incessant chemical actions that new uncouth wines gradually, and after a number of years, grow into comely, mature, well-balanced, perfect wines.

The principal need for a well-bred, well-made young wine to become perfect is peace and time.

But it is not enough for a wine to be perfect in itself; it must be made available for the many thirsty and appreciative Champagne lovers all the world over. And there again the skill and resourcefulness of the Champagne shipper must needs show itself.

When all the available sugar within each Champagne bottle has been disposed of by the natural process of fermentation, the wine has become bright again, but only because its sediment has settled down, and is no longer floating about in the wine itself. This sediment is made up of mineral salts and vegetable matters rejected as useless or harmful during the process of ageing. Should the bottle be stood up or opened, this sediment will again foul the wine. It must go!

In order to get rid of the sediment, each bottle is placed in an almost horizontal position, neck first, on peculiarly constructed sloping tables, and, during a number of weeks, it is slightly shaken and tilted over a little further daily until it is in an almost vertical position neck downwards.

The result of this long, difficult and costly handling is to cause the sediment within the bottle to slide gradually down and eventually to settle altogether upon the inside face of the cork.

When this result has been achieved, the neck of the bottle is placed in a freezing machine, which makes it possible to remove the cork, and with it a small lump of dirty ice; this contains a little wine, and all the sediment which was in the wine. The wine is then ready to be sent to any part of the world; it is both brilliantly clear and naturally sparkling, and it will remain so even under the most trying conditions.

Of course, the first cork which was used when the wine was first bottled is no longer of any use after it has been drawn, some three or more years later, when the wine must be freed from its sediment. A new and even finer cork must be used before the bottle can be sent away into the world on its errand of peace and joy.

But before this second cork is put in, the wine may or may not be sweetened, according to the taste of the people to whom it is destined.

There is no need to add any such sweetening: all Champagne is naturally quite dry or '*brut*' dry, and when no sweetening whatever is added, the Champagne may rightly be shipped as *Nature* or *Brut*. In such a case the wine requires to be kept longer as the natural acidity to which Champagne owes its intense cleanness on the palate requires time to disappear when not covered up by added sugar.

When a little sweetening is added to the wine before it is re-corked, it is entitled to be shipped as *Extra Sec* or Extra Dry. The labels '*Sec*' and 'Dry' no longer convey any idea of a truly dry Champagne; they are used for wines shipped mostly to foreign countries with a sufficiently large addition of sweetening liqueur to make them palatable when served at the end of a meal with ices or sweets.

Whether Champagne be sweetened or not, as soon as the sediment has been removed, it is corked again, the cork is fastened securely with wire, and it is then ready for consumption.

When its marching orders arrive, each bottle is sent up to the light of day above ground, thoroughly washed, dried and dressed.

The dressing consists chiefly of foil and label.

The foil is a thin sheet of tin or pewter paper, gilt, silver or of any colour, which served originally to protect from damp and rats the string used to tie down corks before wire was used for the purpose.

The label is the signature of the shipper responsible for the quality and style of the wine.

When the bottle has been dressed up in foil and label or labels, it is wrapped up in a sheet of thin paper, destined to protect the newly gummed labels from the straw envelope which is then clapped upon it.

Then the bottles in their thick straw jackets are laid in a stout case in two layers of six, neck to punt, and they are ready for shipment to all parts of the world.

Champagne, when good, is undoubtedly better than any other sparkling wine: it costs more and is worth more, but it has ceased to enjoy what was for a long time a monopoly. Methods and devices used for the first time and perfected in the Champagne district may easily be copied and applied elsewhere. Sparkling Champagne owes its unchallenged superiority over all other sparkling wines to characteristics due to purely local conditions, to the soil, climate, aspect and variety of the Champagne vineyards.

For a long time Champagne had remained a ladies' wine, a sweet wine to be sipped at the end of a banquet or with sweets. It was not until the wines of 1857 were shipped that a general reaction set in, in favour of lighter and drier Champagnes. The vintage 1865 was the first to be shipped as very dry, but the wines shipped under this label were far from being truly dry. When, however, the 1874 vintage was shipped, some shippers had been reconciled to the idea of shipping really dry Champagne, and they never had any cause to regret it.

Champagne, truly dry Champagne, became the fashion when the famous wines of the 1874, 1884, 1889 vintages were shipped; it had completely ceased by that time to be a dessert wine; it had become then, and it has remained ever since, a dinner wine, a wine to drink and not to sip, a wine which could and should be served from the beginning and right through the dinner without being stinted.

Many people who drink Champagne, and many more who merely hear or read about it, look upon this most delightful of sparkling wines as a costly luxury only to be indulged in on festive occasions.

Yet Champagne is not merely a wine for banquets and festive occasions; it is even more the wine for the end of a tiring day, for the weak, for the depressed, and for all those who require, as most of us do at some time or other, the fillip, the help, and the joy of this beautiful wine.

II. SPARKLING WINES OTHER THAN CHAMPAGNE

There are many kinds of sparkling wines made in all parts of the world where grapes grow, as well as where they do not grow, as in England, for instance. All such wines are made according to one or the other of three different methods: (1) the Champagne method; (2) the tank method; and (3) the aerated method.

(1) The Champagne method consists in filling bottles with a

wine which is going to finish its fermentation in the said bottle, thus producing its own carbonic acid gas, which cannot escape into the air because the cork in the neck of the bottle has been securely clamped on. When the wine has finished fermenting, the sediment inside the bottle is removed by the Champagne method of *dégorgement*, and the bottle is given a fresh cork, after much or little sugar has been added to the wine to make it more toothsome.

(2) The tank method is the mass-production adaptation of the Champagne method. The wine, instead of being made to ferment in individual bottles, each one having to be securely corked and cleared of its sediment eventually, is allowed to ferment in a large tank, holding the equivalent of thousands of bottles, and so hermetically sealed that the carbonic gas produced by fermentation cannot escape; it is used at the time of the bottling of the wine, which can thus claim to be naturally sparkling insomuch as it is its own carbonic acid gas which is responsible for the bubbles. As all the sediment, the inevitable by-product of fermentation, is left at the bottom of the tank, there is no need of any *dégorgement*, thus effecting a considerable saving in time and labour. Sparkling wines prepared in this way are or ought to be appreciably cheaper than the others, but they are never so good, that is to say, to the trained palate. They stand to Champagne proper in the same relation as Havana cigars cured and rolled at Trenton, when compared to those cured and rolled in Cuba.

(3) The aerated method is a very simple one: it consists in pumping the right quantity of carbonic acid gas into any wine, just as it is done for aerated waters. Such wines have bubbles in plenty, when they are first opened, but they fall flat much more rapidly than the other two sorts of sparkling wines. You can drink these, the cheapest sort of sparkling wines, without any ill-effects and even with pleasure, when you know no better, but they are as British cigars to the true Havanas, a different proposition.

Here is a list of some of the principal sparkling wines, other than Champagne.

ASTI SPUMANTE This is the best known, although not necessarily the best of the sparkling wines made in Italy. It is made from the Moscato grape grown in the vineyards of Asti and others in the same district of Piedmont. It is a white wine, invariably sweet and sometimes very sweet.

BURGUNDY There is a large quantity of wines – white, pink and red – made into sparkling wines in Burgundy, but by far the more popular sort is the Red Sparkling Burgundy; it is usually rather too sweet to be served at any time except at the end of the meal with the sweets or dessert.

HOCKS AND MOSELLES Sparkling Hocks and Moselles have been popular in England for fully a hundred years. Some of them are made from grapes grown in well-known German vineyards and they are sold under the name of their native vineyard; they are made in the same manner as Champagne, and they are much the best of all the German sparkling wines, but they represent a small proportion only of the total output. By far the largest proportion of German sparkling wines are made from imported still wines which are made sparkling, in Germany, sometimes by the *Méthode champenoise* but more often by the cheaper tank (*Cuve close*) system or by an even more modern method. All such sparkling wines are sold under the name of *Sekt*, and its popularity is such that there were some eighty million bottles of Sekt consumed in Germany in 1961.

SAUMUR The name of a charming little French town on the right bank of the Loire, and also the name of the white sparkling wine made from the many vineyards of the district.

Many sparkling wines, mostly sweet or very sweet, are also made in various parts of France, at Bordeaux, both in the Médoc (*Royal Médoc*) (*Clos des Cordeliers*), Arbois, Vouvray, etc.; also many more in Portugal, Spain, Italy, Switzerland, the Crimea, Algeria, South Africa, Australia and the United States, both from the Finger Lakes vineyards, in the State of New York, and from the vineyards of California.

III. TOKAY

The wines of Tokay take their name from the village of Tokaj, in the Hegyalja district of north-eastern Hungary, at the foot of the Carpathians. The best Tokay wine is known as *Tokaij Essencia*, the next best as *Tokaij Aszu*, which is not quite so rich, but very sweet and of greatly concentrated flavour. Both will keep longer than any other wine, and both deserve Professor George Saintsbury's verdict: 'No more a wine but a prince of Liqueurs.' The next grade is called *Tokaij Szamorodner*: it is more of a table wine, and fairly dry, unless made in a particularly hot year, when it is quite rich and is then labelled, *Tokaij édes szamorodner*.

The Table Wines of
Non-European Vineyards

There are much greater quantities of red table wines now made
from grapes grown in the Americas, Africa and Oceania than
ever before, chiefly because the demand is greater. But it may
also be said that the demand for table wines, red, white and
rosé, is greater chiefly due to the fact that their quality is better
than ever before. Much progress has been made in wine
technology to the benefit of all wines, but the control of
temperature has been of greater importance to the wines of
non-European vineyards because in most, if not in all of them,
the vintage takes place – that is, the grapes are picked and pressed
– when the weather is still very hot, and there were formerly no
means to check the fermentation coming on much too fast for
the good of the wine. Today, thanks to the control of temperature, the tempo of fermentation in the Barossa Valley of South
Australia or the western province of the Cape can be exactly the
same as in the Médoc or on the Rhine.

UNITED STATES OF AMERICA The only good red
table wines made in North America are made from grapes of
fine quality grown in northern California, that is north of San
Francisco, mostly in the Napa Valley, the Livermore Valley,
Sonoma, Santa Cruz, Santa Clara and a few other counties.
They represent less than twenty per cent of the total production
of table wines of California. The best of them are usually sold
under the name of their native vineyard as well as under the
name of the grape from which they were 'mostly' made, such
as Cabernet or Pinot Noir. 'Mostly' means that there was not
less than fifty-one per cent of Cabernet grape in the red table
wine offered for sale under that name; but although the name

will be the same on the label, the wine in the bottle will be a much better wine if made from seventy-five or one hundred per cent Cabernet.

Since the Repeal of the Volstead Act in 1933, that is when Prohibition came to an end in the U.S.A., the quantity of grapes grown and wines made in the U.S.A. has risen rapidly from year to year to keep abreast of the growing demand of the American consumer. Although the demand and the supply of the cheaper and lower quality wines is much greater in the U.S.A. as everywhere else, the standard of quality of the red table wines of California is now higher than it was before Prohibition.

California is the most important wine-producing state of the U.S.A. but there are grapes grown and some wine made in a dozen other states: upon a fairly important scale in New York and Ohio, but to a very limited extent elsewhere. There is, however, a very great difference between most of the wines of California and most of the wines made from grapes of the eastern vineyards, a difference of smell and taste, bouquet and flavour, due to the fact that the wines of California are made from European species of grapes, and the others from native American species.

CANADA   In spite of winters which are too long, and summers which are too short, Canada grows some wine-making grapes commercially and produces a limited quantity of wines from poor to fair in quality.

MEXICO   has had vineyards since the first Spanish missionaries brought the vine and introduced viticulture to the land in the sixteenth century. There are a great many red table wines and other wines being made every year in Mexico, but most of them, if not all, are rather below than above the *ordinaire* standard of quality.

SOUTH AMERICA   The three countries of South America in which there are important vineyards and where much wine is made are the Argentine Republic, Chile and Brazil. A fair amount of wine is also made in Uruguay, much less in Peru and less still in Bolivia.

Argentina. In the Argentine the most extensive vineyards and the greatest wineries are in the westernmost part of the country, as far as Mendoza and San Juan, before the great Andes mountains are reached. The home demand for quality Argentine wines is small and so therefore is their supply. The majority of Argentine table wines are very reasonably priced and they have a better claim to being called good value than good wines.

Chile produces some table wines of fine quality, mostly from the vineyards of the Central zone, not a great deal below the top mountain vineyards, but well above the vineyards of the foothills of the Andes. All the wines of Chile are made from European grapes, some of them from the choicest species, that is the species responsible for the best wines. Chile also has the benefit of a rainfall which is, as a rule, sufficient, whereas in the Argentine most vineyards have to be irrigated. There is also in Chile a better wine-making tradition dating back to the first Basque *vignerons* from Spain. The good beverage wines of Chile are greatly appreciated in Chile itself, and they are also in demand in the U.S.A. and in a number of other markets in competition with the good wines of other nations.

Brazil has produced wine for a long time past in the Saõ Paulo region. However, far more extensive vineyards have been planted more recently in the southernmost provinces of the country, where very large quantities of poor quality wine is now being made.

AFRICA *North Africa.* The Egyptians grew grapes and made wine long before Rome was built, and there are still some grapes grown in the Nile Delta, and some wine made there by Italians. All the important vineyards of North Africa, however, are farther west, beyond Libya, from Tunisia along the whole of the Mediterranean seaboard of North Africa to Morocco and the Atlantic. In many parts of Algeria, but chiefly in the regions of Algiers and Oran, many thousands of acres, planted as vineyards by the French before the Arab takeover of Algeria in 1962, produced considerable quantities of wine including a great many red table wines; practically all of these wines were exported, chiefly to France, and blended with French red table wines lacking in either colour or alcoholic strength, or both.

South Africa. There are still grapes growing and there is still wine being made before and beyond Constantia, a few miles from Cape Town. The first South African vineyard was planted there late in the seventeenth century by the first Dutch Governor at the Cape. Most, however, not to say very nearly all, of the rapidly rising quantity of South African wines come from the western province of the Cape and many vineyards further north.

The best table wines of South Africa come from the many vineyards of the Paarl Valley, and right and left of them beyond Stellenbosch as far as Somerset West on one side and Tulbagh on the opposite side. S.A.W.F.A., the South African Wine Farmers' Association, has been given powers which might well be called despotic, but it has used them so wisely for the good of *vignerons* and the wine trade of South Africa, that the demand for Cape wines is steadily growing, both in South Africa and throughout the world.

AUSTRALASIA *Australia* has probably benefited to a greater extent than all other vinelands from the progress of wine technology, a fair share of which was due to the late Professor Fornachon, a very remarkable Australian oenologist, in charge of the South Australia Wine Institute at Adelaide.

The vineyards of South Australia have been fortunate so far to be free from phylloxera, and they produce more wine than the vineyards of the other states of Australia. The oldest of the South Australian vineyards are the few remaining Metropolitan vineyards which are still in production. Most of them were so near Adelaide that they were doomed to disappear under the rising tide of brick and mortar, homes, shops and factories, which paid a better dividend than grapes. Most of the important vineyards of South Australia are either seawards or south of Adelaide, or to the north, northwards of that city, along the Barossa Valley and a good way beyond it. They produce great quantities of good quality table wines, as well as every other kind of wine and spirits.

The vineyards of New South Wales are the oldest in Australia and those of the Hunter River Valley still produce much wine, some of which constitute the finest table wines of Australia.

The vineyards of Victoria which produce the greatest quantity of wine are those of the Murray River. They are responsible for a large proportion of fortified wines and for the best of Australia's sparkling wines.

The vineyards of Western Australia, north of Perth, were planted more recently than those of the preceding three states, but they are now making good progress as regards both the quantity and quality of their wines. The same cannot be said of the vineyards of Queensland.

New Zealand. Although grapes have been grown and wine has been made in New Zealand on a very limited scale since the early part of the nineteenth century, there are now important vineyards in the North Islands, chiefly in the Auckland and Napier regions. The more important vineyards of the Auckland or western side of the island are those of Henderson, while those of the eastern side are immediately south of Napier in the Hawkes Bay area.

Postscript: The Wine Connoisseur

The connoisseur

What is a connoisseur? A connoisseur is one who knows and loves that which is good, beautiful, uncommon, interesting; everything that is the best of its kind and, above all, genuine.

To become a connoisseur one must be keen and one must be trained.

Many can see who do not appreciate beauty any more than a cow looking at the most glorious sunset.

Many can hear who do not appreciate harmony any more than a dog in an organ loft.

Many can taste what they drink who are interested as much in the quantity of the supply and as little in its quality as some of the animals at the Zoo.

Pictures, music and wine may be good, bad or indifferent; it is all the same to those who cannot see, hear or taste; and it is very nearly the same to those unfortunate people who do not see, hear or taste with the keen, apprehensive, appreciative mind of the connoisseur.

The connoisseur must possess a lively sense of appreciation and be guided by good taste. Good taste is nobody's monopoly, and different people may have good taste who have not the same tastes.

The connoisseur must neither give up his individuality nor fall into eccentricities; he must cultivate the sense of measure, of true proportion, which is the hallmark of good taste.

The connoisseur must be prepared to make mistakes; they are inevitable, they should be helpful, and they must not make him lose confidence in his judgement.

The connoisseur must be critical and not take for granted

that the expert is always right; but he must not be self-opinionated and refuse advice.

The connoisseur must not be extravagant or hasty; but he must still less be mean or casual.

The connoisseur must school himself to resist temptation; he must learn to go without that which he cannot afford and to leave alone fakes, doubtful bargains, and 'just-as-good' substitutes which cost less and are worthless.

The Wine Connoisseur

The wine connoisseur is one who knows good wine from bad and who appreciates the distinctive merits of different wines.

The wine connoisseur drinks wine in moderation, but regularly and appreciatively. It is excess – not habit – which blunts appreciation.

A little wine every day costs very little money and is the safest, as well as the pleasantest, tonic for body and mind alike. But wine, whatever its name, its age or its cost must be honest if it is to be good and to do good.

How can you tell good wine from bad; how can you become a wine connoisseur?

By using your senses and your common sense. By looking at wine, smelling it and tasting it with critical eyes, nose and palate before committing it to your veins and your brain.

Look at your wine critically: it must be not only clear but brilliant, be it ruby or amber, young or old, cheap or dear. If it is dull or thick, reject it; if bright, let it go before the tribunal of your nose.

Smell your wine critically: it must be clean-smelling. If you can detect the slightest mouldy, foul smell, or some unnatural, artificial scent, however faint, leave it alone. If its discreet aroma is pleasant, remain a while with bowed head over your glass; try to remember the occasion when you last met the same charming bouquet and what was the name of the wine.

Then you may send your wine to the next court where your palate awaits it.

Taste your wine critically: it must be clean and pleasant. If you detect any unsavoury, sour or merely suspicious taste, spit it out as you would a bad oyster or a piece of tainted meat. But if the wreath of tiny taste-buds of your tongue and palate receive your wine joyfully, pause but one instant, again to search your memory for the name and vintage of the wine you are drinking, and then swallow it gratefully.

How to Buy Wine

Wine is the living blood of the grape; it possesses life; it is liable to sickness and doomed to death.

Never buy any wine – be its price ever so cheap or its name ever so famous – which is not sound. A sound wine is a healthy wine: health alone is harmony.

The best wine for you to buy is the wine which suits you best, not the wine which it suits somebody to sell to you.

Buy wine from a wine merchant with a reputation to lose.

Never buy a wine as a speculation: it is not safe.

Never buy any wine that you do not care for, and do not buy more of any wine than you are likely to require.

When tempted, be wary lest you fall! Bargains are not safe: it is better to pay more and buy less; but buy well.

When buying wine, place quality first, variety second, quantity third, and cost last. Always buy some cheap, new, sound beverage wines even if you can afford to buy the most expensive wines as well.

Buy cheap wines to drink habitually and fine wines to drink occasionally.

Trust your wine merchant or leave him. Train your palate so that you may trust your own judgement; but find a wine merchant whom you can trust as well.

Buy fair wine and treat it fairly. Find a home for it – a cool, dark and quiet home: a good cellar.

How to Keep Wine

A good cellar should be underground, but well ventilated, cool in summer and winter alike, and scrupulously clean.

When wine is delivered to you, remove straw envelopes and paper wrappings: examine every bottle and reject faulty ones.

Never lay down a bottle of wine which shows signs of 'ullage' – that is to say, the cork of which has allowed some of the wine to ooze out.

All wines should be binned in a horizontal position, so that the whole of the inside face of the cork is constantly in contact with the liquid, failing which the corks will shrink, some air will find its way into the bottle, and the wine will be spoilt.

If you are so short of cellar space that you cannot bin away your Champagne or other cased wines as soon as you receive them, be careful to see that the cases are lying flat and not on their sides; otherwise the bottles inside the case would be in a vertical instead of in a horizontal position; half of them would be neck downwards and safe, but the other half would be standing up and likely to grow flat after a time.

When binning Port, see to it that the white splash on the bottles is always uppermost: it will then be in exactly the same position as before it reached your cellar, and the crust, which is bound to be disturbed by the moving, will settle down much better into the old grooves which it has made for itself in the very metal of the bottle.

Watch your bins of wine. Be on the look-out for any weepers so as to remove them and use them quickly before they have become ullages.

Wine needs, and repays, care. Wine deserves not the hireling's care, but that loving care which is the only care that is intelligent and worthy of so precious a gift as Wine.

How to Serve Wine

Decanting. Wine should always be served in brilliant condition.

All red wines with bottle-age throw a sediment which fouls

the wine if it passes from the bottle into the glass. All such red wines should be carefully decanted.

Whenever possible, decant your old wine in the cellar, straight from the bin.

Take the bottle gently from the bin and lay it softly in a cradle.

Remove the metal cap or the wax protecting the outside face of the cork.

Wipe the lower lip of the bottle all round and thoroughly with a clean cloth.

Drive your corkscrew slowly right through the centre of the cork and draw the cork steadily without any jerks, without either haste or hesitation.

Once the cork is drawn, wipe the inside lip of the bottle with a clean cloth, take hold of the bottle firmly in your right hand, and SLOWLY pour its contents into a decanter held in your left hand.

Place a lighted candle or an electric bulb behind the shoulder of the bottle and watch the wine as it passes out of the neck of the bottle. As soon as you see some loose sediment come to the neck of the bottle, stand the bottle up. What wine is left in the bottle is unfit for consumption; it is far better to lose a little wine and much sediment than to spoil a decanter of good wine with a little sediment.

Do not serve wine from basket or cradle if you can help it. It is always better to decant it.

The temperature at which you will serve your fine wines is of great importance.

Temperature. Avoid extremes: use neither fire nor ice; shocks are always bad for wine.

White wines should be served cold; they may be iced, but no ice should ever be put in the wine itself.

Red wines should be served at the temperature of the dining-room. They will be spoilt if warmed up quickly, either by being dipped into hot water or placed near the fire.

Decant old Claret one hour, and old Port two or three hours

before dinner. Let them stand in the dining-room, where they will take the temperature of the room.

Glasses. Never serve fine wines – or fine brandy – in small glasses. Use large glasses, but never let them be filled to the brim. The subtle bouquet of a wine is its greatest charm, but you will never be able to appreciate it should your glass be too small or too full.

Fine glasses materially add to the enjoyment of fine wines: they enable one to appreciate its brilliant colour. Above all, it is absolutely indispensable that both decanters and glasses should be faultlessly clean. The cloth used to wipe and polish glasses should never be used for anything else; the finest wine will be completely ruined if served in glasses which have been wiped with a dirty cloth.

The order in which wines should be served varies according to individual tastes and the food served. The usually accepted order, however, is as follows:

With oysters, Chablis or Dry Champagne. With soup, pale Sherry or Dry Madeira. With fish, Champagne or dry white wines. With entrées, Claret. With roast or game, Burgundy. With sweets, Sauternes. With dessert, Port, Brown Sherry or rich Madeira. With cheese every kind of wine is acceptable, which is why Grimod de la Reynière called cheese *le biscuit des ivrognes.*

General Index

Index of Chateaux, Vineyards etc.

More about Penguins
and Pelicans

Penguinews, which appears every month, contains
details of all the new books issued by Penguins
as they are published. From time to time it is
supplemented by *Penguins in Print*, which is a
complete list of all titles available. (There are some
five thousand of these.)

A specimen copy of *Penguinews* will be sent to
you free on request. For a year's issues (including
the complete lists) please send 50p if you live in
the British Isles, or 75p if you live elsewhere.
Just write to Dept EP, Penguin Books Ltd,
Harmondsworth, Middlesex, enclosing a cheque
or postal order, and your name will be added to
the mailing list.

In the U.S.A.: For a complete list of books
available from Penguin in the United States write
to Dept CS, Penguin Books Inc., 7110
Ambassador Road, Baltimore, Maryland 21207.

In Canada: For a complete list of books available
from Penguin in Canada write to Penguin Books
Canada Ltd, 41 Steelcase Road West, Markham,
Ontario.

Another Penguin Handbook

Cooking with Wine

Robin McDouall

'I have written about cooking with wine because there
are some people who think there is something
mysterious about cooking with wine, something
un-English . . . I have tried to show, in a series of mainly
simple recipes, that there is nothing odder about using
wine as an ingredient than butter, eggs, flour, or, getting
rather more way-out, garlic or tarragon.'

Robin McDouall entertained us with his previous
Penguin, *Cookery Book for the Greedy*. Here, as ever, he
is unfailingly expert and urbane, whether marinating or
poaching. He'll persuade you to use that bottom inch of
vin blanc to make Mushrooms in Wine Vinaigrette –
and you'll soon be stocking a cellar for Coquilles
Saint-Jacques au vin blanc and Poulet Sauté Bagatelle.
And then there are Rognons Sautés au Madère, Fried
Pork a Marinheira, and, to follow, Apples Fort Belvedere
(Cox's Orange Pippins in rum). You'll be surprised
at the delicious number of ways you can disguise
Calvados, Sherry, Champagne, Kirsch, beer and cider.